Indira Gandhi
A Political Biography
(1966–1984)

Indira Gandhi
A Political Biography
(1966–1984)

Benny Aguiar

Vitasta

Let Knowledge Spread

Times
Group
Books

Published by
Renu Kaul Verma for
Vitasta Publishing Pvt. Ltd.
2/15, First Floor, Ansari Road, Daryaganj,
New Delhi - 110 002
info@vitastapublishing.com

Reprint 2012
ISBN 978-93-80828-62-6 (PB)

© 2007, Benny Aguiar
ISBN 81-89766-11-2 (HB)

Typeset by Vitasta Publishing Pvt. Ltd.
Printed at Saurabh Printers Pvt. Ltd., New Delhi
Cover design by Prabha Singh

Marketed and Distributed exclusively in India & Sub-Continent by:

Times Group Books
(A division of Bennett, Coleman and Company Limited)
Times Annexe, Express Building
9-10 Bahadur Shah Zafar Marg, New Delhi-110 002

Contents

Preface

A study of Indira Gandhi's life and times is always a subject of interest because of the panaroma it provides to students of Indian politics and the society.

Let me, however, say that this is not a biography of Indira Gandhi. It is rather a chronicle of the years between 1966 and 1984, barring the period between 1977–79, during which she was the prime minister. It is a historical study of the tumultuous events, conflicting forces and trends during the period that shaped the course of our post-independence history. It tries to find out what lessons they hold for the country's future. I have tried to piece together these momentous events into an integral narrative so that it reads like a biography.

I have tried to analyse the underlying causes that led to the unfolding of these events. These causes were intricate and numerous, interacting with each other. They were social and political, moral and religious, economical and cultural. Caste and creed, language and region, party loyalties and personality clashes, all played their part in shaping the course of the country's history. Not to let the divisive forces get out of hand and play havoc with the development of the country should be the endeavour of all who have the interests of India at heart.

What then are the momentous events during Indira Gandhi's premiership that have shaped the history of the country? I have tried to capture the events after she became the prime minister following the demise of Lal Bahadur Shastri in 1966. This includes events such as her winning of the mandate to rule the country, the unmaking of Pakistan, the birth of Bangladesh, the exodus of refugees from East Pakistan, the war between India and Pakistan, JP's total revolution, the Emergency, the rise and fall of Janata Party, Operation Blue Star and her assassination on 31 October 1984. These events shook the country and the subcontinent and left an indelible mark on Indian history.

On the subject of the refugees from East Pakistan, I was particularly well placed to give a first hand eye witness account since I visited Tripura, Salt Lake City near Calcutta's Dum Dum Airport and the Road to Petrapole on the Bangladesh border when the refugees were pouring into India by the hundreds of thousands.

Whether or not Nehru wanted Indira to be his immediate successor and start a dynasty is debatable. But what Nehru and Indira and to a certain extent, Rajiv had in common was an immense popular appeal. So, they became the darlings of the masses. Certainly, both Nehru and Indira were srong willed and could hold the country together as none others could.

It was Nehru's singular contribution that India became a "secular" state. Nehru's ideas of secularism may have been somewhat different from those of Gandhiji. While the latter believed that all religions were equal and should be given equal respect (*sarva dharma sambhava*), Nehru's secularism was derived more from the Western ideas of the separation of religion from the state. Religion, Nehru believed, was a personal matter and should not be allowed to interfere with the governance of the country.

Indira Gandhi was a firm believer in secularism. She introduced the words 'secular' and 'socialist' into the Preamble of the Constitution, through 44th Amendment Act of 1976, which describes India as a "sovereign, socialist, secular and democratic republic."

The events during Indira's time left a deep impression on her life and character just as her own personality had a dominant influence on shaping those events. These events projected her as a woman of courage and tenacity, determination and will.

Even Atal Behari Vajpayee likened her to Hindu Goddess Durga. She was a woman who loved her country and its people with an enduring and passionate love just as they, in their turn, admired and adored her. She had some fatal flaws in her character: a tendency to identify the country's interests with her own and to be a democrat as well as a dictator. She soon became a role model for the country.

Most of the following pages are based on articles I wrote for the *Tablet*, London, of which I was the Bombay correspondent for nearly 30 years and on editorials in *The Examiner* of which I was editor for as many years. I have pieced them all together to make a continuous narrative which should interest the student of history as well as the general reader.

— **Benny Aguiar**

Acknowledgement

My thanks are due to Mr John Wilkins, till recently Editor of the *Tablet*, London, who edited and published my articles about India which have gone into the making of this book.

My thanks are also due to Mr J Paul de Souza, Editor of *Chemical Age* for his valuable suggestions and Mr Ralph Sanfrancis, who typed the manuscript.

ONE

In a Great Tradition

When 48-year-old Indira Gandhi was selected to be India's third prime minister and leader of her 460 million people, eyebrows were raised and questions asked if there was no outstanding and capable man to fill the post. India was at a turning point in its history.

After conducting vigorously the second war against Pakistan, India's second prime minister, Lal Bahadur Shastri, had gone to Tashkent, and with the help of the Russians concluded a peace agreement with Pakistan. Tragedy struck. He never returned; he died in Tashkent on 11 January 1966. The conflict with Pakistan had put the country back by at least twenty years. Meanwhile, due to a severe drought the spectre of famine loomed large over the land. Would a fragile woman be able to meet the challenges that faced the country?

Critics overlooked the fact that Indira Gandhi was heir to a great tradition. She was Jawaharlal Nehru's daughter. He strode the country like a colossus. S K Patil, a former mayor of Bombay, said of him that he was like a giant banyan tree, under which nothing could grow. None of the country's leaders, even in the Congress, could hold a candle to Nehru, so towering was his personality. But Indira was his daughter. She was schooled in politics and the art and culture, not so much by tutors as by Nehru himself. It was for her that he wrote, *Discovery of India* and *Glimpses of World History*, in the shape of letters from a father to his daughter while he was in prison. Hostess to her father's numerous and important visitors and as a constant companion during his travels abroad, Indira kept house for him and became his mentor during the later years of his life when he increasingly sought her advice on matters of policy. She was also a woman and political leader in her own right, of courage and determination. She had played her part in the Independence struggle and gone to prison along with her father when the 'Quit India' movement was launched. Rising to be the president of the Congress party in 1959, she was instrumental in ousting the Communist Party's rule in Kerala and in the bifurcation of Bombay State into Gujarat and Maharashtra.

Minister of Broadcasting and Information in Lal Bahadur Shastri's Cabinet, Indira's victory over Morarji Desai in a straight contest for the leadership of the country represented the victory of the progressive and forward looking bloc in the nationalist movement over the rigid and conservative section of the Congress Party, which however still commanded a sizable minority as the results of the election showed. The need of the hour was to lead the country out of the slough of despond where it had settled after Shastri's death, and on the road to agricultural and general prosperity. In carrying out that task Indira as her asset had her father's and her own tremendous appeal to the masses. In Between father and daughter, Jawaharlal and Indira, straddled the first 50 years of India's Independence which influenced the course of history as none other had done.

TWO

A Difficult Start

The mood of the country, when Indira Gandhi took over as prime minister on 24 January 1966, was sombre. Lal Bahadur Shastri's death had cast a pall of gloom over the land and the Republic Day celebrations were deliberately muted.

More serious was the economic situation. Indira Gandhi admitted in her Republic Day broadcast that the months to come were to bristle with difficulties. The rains had failed, there was drought in many parts, agricultural production had suffered a sharp decline; economic aid from abroad and export earnings had fallen short of expectations; industrial production had been hurt due to lack of foreign exchange.

The first duty of her government, Indira said, was to ensure food to her people. President Sarvepalli Radhakrishnan, too, in his broadcast message called for an all-out food drive and wanted the new government to attend to the problem immediately.

Indira Gandhi set about tackling the problem as soon as she took office. By integrating community development and cooperation into the Ministry of Food and Agriculture and placing it all into the experienced hands of C Subramaniam, who played a vital role during the green revolution, she provided the means to give a greater sense of urgency and practical orientation to community development projects.

More significantly, she appointed Ashoka Mehta, an expert economist and deputy chairman of the Planning Commission, the minister of Planning. This ensured that the decisions were executed and duplication and waste of men and money was avoided. These appointments reflected Indira's sense of realism and her determination to put first things first and close the gap between intent and action. But, Indira Gandhi was still young and lacked the experience of her father. Four months later she took a decision that brought down her political rating. She pegged down the value of the rupee in terms of foreign currency by 36.5 per cent. Doubtless, it was a bold attempt to look at the economy of the country squarely in the face, an act of courage and hardheaded realism. In the black market the rupee had already been unofficially devalued. But it was also an abject confession of failure on the part of the government and a sad commentary on the parlous state of the country's economy.

Quite clearly the country had been living beyond its means; its investments in grandiose projects and on mammoth schemes had not borne the fruit expected of them; it had been borrowing lavishly and not repaying the loans and had therefore to be declared near-insolvent. True, there had been factors beyond its control, like the drought and the war with Pakistan but ultimately the fault lay with the government and the country's planners.

The consequences of devaluation were predictable—prices began soaring. The price of gold, silver and imports mounted. Not long before the price of consumer goods also began to rise. Even if these consumer goods were produced domestically, the capital goods or the raw material for many of them was imported. The foreign debt repayment became costlier. The economy was so tied up with foreign aid, that an all-round increase in prices was bound to result sooner or later. This increase in the price spiral led to an increase in demand for wages and thus paved way for inflation.

Would Indira Gandhi be able to keep her promise to keep prices down, especially of essential and consumer goods? The only answer was increased agricultural and industrial production. Without it devaluation would prove to be nothing but a gimmick that brought untold hardships and misery on millions.

Unfortunately, for Indira Gandhi, the state of the country's economy appeared to be like that of a sick man getting worse. Shortly before the general elections on 16 November 1966, she went on the air, telling her people that they faced yet another year of famine.

There had been severe drought in Bihar, Uttar Pradesh, Madhya Pradesh, Maharashtra, Gujarat and West Bengal. She gave a heart-rending picture of the rural scene in those areas of Bihar and Uttar Pradesh, which she had recently visited. Countless millions of people, she said, have had the bread snatched out of their mouths by an abnormal failure of rain from mid-August onwards. 'Green fields that promised an abundant harvest have withered. The grain has died on the stalk. The toil and the sweat of months have been reduced to dust. There is hunger and distress in millions of homes.'

During her visit the prime minister wept at the sight of tribals living off roots, 'Yet,' she said, 'I saw many fields ploughed in the hope of rain... Thousands of wells are being dug or deepened. Lift irrigation schemes are being put into operation to pump water from rivers to irrigate as large an area as possible... Driving through Monghyar District I saw a peasant watering a tiny ploughed field with a bucket and a *lota*. This is symbolic of the heroic effort and spirit of our people. Whatever their suffering, they are not defeated.' Indira pleaded that the food problem be taken out of party politics.

THREE

Congress:
The Cracked Monolith

Was Indira's *cri de coeur* just an attempt to bolster her party's sagging fortunes or a cover-up for its shortcomings? It was not. Indeed, Jayaprakash Narayan had called the unprecedented drought a greater calamity than the Bihar earthquake of 1934. But as the elections approached and the Congress published its manifesto, the party could only offer the same old mixture as before, only in larger doses: more socialism, more taxation, more place for the public sector, more emphasis on industry and a bigger, bolder Plan.

True, the record of Congress' achievements appeared impressive, at least on paper. There had been the beginning of a scientific and industrial revolution, it was claimed; during the 15 years of the three Five-Year Plans five times more steel and cement, nine times more petroleum products and 15 times more fertiliser were registered. Around 52,300 villages received electricity as against 3,700 in 1950–51. Five lakh pumps were installed, seven lakh wells dug and

48 million more acres of land irrigated. Cloth production doubled and food production more than doubled. People were earning more, eating more and living longer. Average workers' income had risen from Rs 383 to Rs 1,475 and per capita food consumption from 12.8 ounces a day to 15.4. Three times more children were going to school and there was double the number of hospitals. Average life span was now 50 years, compared to 32 earlier.

The questions, however, still remained. Was the progress proportionate to the capital invested in the plans? Did it provide for a decent standard of living? Two ounces more of food would hardly make much difference to a poor man's diet. Because of the emphasis on heavy industry and the neglect of agriculture, India's hungry millions still went hungry. There had been a 70 per cent rise in prices between 1961 and 1966. Deficit financing had led to inflation and this in turn to devaluation. Would a bigger, bolder Plan, involving an outlay of Rs 23,750 crore bring about the required increase in production?

In all these questions the Swatantra Party manifesto found a useful handle to draw up a strong indictment of 20 years of Congress rule. Agriculture had been neglected but the tempo of industrial and commercial activity was at a low ebb because of the licence-permit *raj*. Deficit financing and devaluation had proved conclusively that the country was insolvent, riven by political, commercial, linguistic and racial factions. Students were up in arms against teachers, tenants against landlords, and workers in industry against employers. Bribery and corruption, inefficiency and favouritism were rampant. There was no clear foreign policy in a haze of talk about non-alignment, coexistence, peace and disarmament. The country was in a shambles, democracy in danger.

The Swatantra Party manifesto presented itself as the Party of Free Enterprise, determined to rid the country of all controls that prevent free competition, opposed to Soviet-style planning, bent on scrapping the Fourth Five-Year Plan, dissolving the Planning Commission, abandoning deficit financing and other inflationary policies, cutting down bureaucratic government expenditure, reducing direct and indirect taxes, restoring law and order, checking corruption, appointing an Ombudsman to go into citizens' grievances and upholding the rule of law and *dharma*, the true basis of enduring moral progress and material prosperity. The manifesto presented the Swatantra Party as a clear-cut alternative to the Congress.

A not-so-clear alternative was the Jana Sangh, the party of Hindu revivalism, which started an agitation for banning cow slaughter on the pretext of implementing the section of the Constitution that provides for legislation on agricultural organisation and animal husbandry.

Crusading to save the cow, thousands of 'holy men', vowed to *ahimsa* (non-violence), went berserk and rampaged through the streets, as they converged on Parliament, causing wanton destruction to life and property. The 'ban cow slaughter' movement appeared more of a political stunt, engineered by the Jana Sangh, to make use of the base, elemental and irrational forces that surface when an appeal is made to blind religious sentiment.

Confusion worsened and the congressmen, who felt themselves cheated by the parent organisation as they had been denied tickets for the elections, launched a new party, the Jana Congress. It had some important names such as those of Humayun Kabir and Hare Krishna Mahatab and the blessings of such national figures as Acharya Kripalani and Jayaprakash Narayan. It was joined in Kerala by the Kerala Congress, which had seceded from the All India Congress because it had given a raw deal particularly to Christians. Efforts at reconciliation, in which Indira Gandhi was involved, failed and the Kerala Congress allied itself with the Swatantra Party.

In West Bengal, the Bangla Congress also seceded because of territorial differences but allied itself with the Left Communists. In its statement, the Jana Congress declared its desire to go back to the ideals of the Congress before Independence, to put an end to jobbery and corruption, make the country more self-sufficient in food through cooperatives and encourage competition between the public and private sector. The only immediate result of the launching of the new party was to add one more party to the Opposition and increase the anarchy and disunity in the country.

The party rivalry, the economic crisis and the caste and communal differences led to some ugly incidents of violence during the campaigns. The elections themselves passed peacefully enough. The results, however, were an absolute debacle for the Congress. Its erstwhile steamroller majority was slashed to the point where only 20 members were needed to cross the floor and bring the Gandhi government down. Opposition parties came to power in nine states: Kerala, Madras, Orissa, Uttar Pradesh, Bihar, Rajasthan, Punjab and West Bengal. The Congress could no longer take itself for granted as the indisputable master of the country and the unique framer of its policies. The monolith had cracked.

Prime cause for the Congress debacle was, of course, the spiralling rise of prices, of food and other essential commodities. Over nearly half of the country, more than half of the electorate had gone to the polls and registered their dissatisfaction with things as they were and their determination not to put up with them any longer. All they asked for were just the bare necessities for an honest decent living, just enough food to keep body and soul together, just enough clothing for protection against the inclemencies of the weather and did not find them.

True enough, India had made some progress since Independence. The average Indian might have been ever so slightly better fed and better clothed. But India still took one of the last places among the developing countries. The Fourth Five-Year Plan asked him to wait till 1972 when the industrial take-off would be achieved. But the results of the elections showed people were not prepared to wait.

There were other causes besides for the disenchantment with the Congress. There was the long and interminable story of graft and corruption that had affected even the highest echelons like a virus and the inability of the Congress to eject it from its midst. There was a steady and voluminous growth of a Himalayan bureaucracy and red tape that allowed full play for the operation of Parkinson's law. There was high-handedness and hubris, the infighting and the manoeuvring for power, the slow arteriosclerosis of a gerontocracy that made it difficult for the Congress to respond to the calls of idealism with the same resilience it displayed in its youth.

The process of Congress disintegration, far from slowing down after the elections, tended to go faster. In the Pondicherry Legislative Assembly, seven members defected, reducing its strength from 20 to 14 in a House of 29.

The Congress Government had to resign. It was a similar story in the newly constituted state of Haryana, where the Congress had won an absolute majority. Thirteen members left the party because they had not been given ministries reducing it to a minority and forcing it to resign. Thus two more states lost to the Congress.

FOUR

Polarisation

Because the basic issue on which the 1966 elections turned was an economic one and 65 per cent of the electorate rejected the Congress for its inability to deliver, there resulted a drift away from the Centre to the Right or the Left and a certain polarisation between the different social and political forces in the country. The Congress itself was a conglomeration of different economic viewpoints, but the result of the conflicting pressures was a middle of the road economic policy, leaning slightly to the Left. The Swatantra Party now emerged as the strongest of the Opposition parties in Parliament having registered considerable gains in Gujarat and Rajasthan and leading a coalition ministry with the Jana Sangh in Orissa.

On the other end of the spectrum were the Communist parties, one Moscow-oriented and the other Peking-oriented. The split in the Indian Communist Party reflected the split in international Communism and proved detrimental to Communist fortunes in

Andhra Pradesh, long regarded as the fertile breeding ground for Left extremism. But their gains in the assemblies in Kerala, West Bengal and the Lok Sabha in general made them once again a force to be reckoned with. Their ultimate aim was the socialisation of property and the nationalisation of the means of production. But whereas the Right or Moscow-oriented Communists were more ready to accept coexistence and to use parliamentary means to foster the class struggle, the Left or Peking-oriented Communists, strove 'for the establishment of a people's democracy by developing a powerful mass revolutionary movement by combining parliamentary and extra parliamentary forms of struggle.' The Right Communists joined hands with the Bangla Congress to form a coalition ministry. But it was in Kerala that both the Communist parties made the most striking gains and were voted to power.

Kerala had gone red. The two Communist parties had won more than half the number of seats in the state assembly. Together with the other members of the United Leftist Front they won 115 of the 133 seats and the result could only be considered as a landslide for the Leftists and an absolute rout for both the official as well as the rebel Congress. History had repeated itself, the lessons of the Great Upsurge unlearned, and the Communists had once again come to power in Kerala, exploiting the grievances of the people and taking advantage of the disunion in the Congress. Only this time it was the Left Communists, led by E M S Namboodiripad who would be entrenched in power.

Very near to the Communist parties in its aims and ideals and closely associated with them in provoking strikes and paralysing civic and economic life was the Samyukta Socialist Party (SSP), which now led a coalition ministry in Bihar and won a sizable number of seats in the Uttar Pradesh Assembly. The SSP was for socialising the property used as a means of production and hiring labour. One important member of this party who won a seat in Parliament was George Fernandes. He trounced the former Railway Minister S K Patil in a hard-hitting contest in Bombay South.

Economic factors were not the only ones influencing the outcome of the elections. The results showed a resurgence of those divisive and centrifugal forces of race, caste and language that had so often before threatened the unity of the country. One of the biggest surprises of the election was the complete rout of the Congress in Madras and the rolling of such eminent heads as those of Kamaraj, the Congress president, and Subramaniam, the former Food Minister.

Madras (now Chennai) state was one of the most efficiently administered and the fact that the DMK (Dravida Munetra Kazhagam) won such a complete victory could only be explained by the appeal it made to the anti-Hindi, anti-Aryan and anti-Brahmin sentiments of the Tamilians. Differences between North and South go back to early Indian history, but their most recent expression was the attempt to force Hindi down the throats of Tamilians and make it the national language. So great was this resentment against what was called Hindi Imperialism that students burnt themselves alive in the streets rather than be forced to learn Hindi in schools and colleges.

On the other hand, there was resurgence and strengthening of the forces of Hindu communalism and revivalism, embodied in the Jana Sangh that had so often in the past been responsible for the agitation against missionaries and was behind the agitation for a ban on cow slaughter to be written into the Constitution. Though the Jana Sangh had no particular economic policy (what policy it had was borrowed from the Swatantra Party), it was so well organised that it succeeded in taking over the Delhi Metropolitan Council and obtaining a sizable number of seats in

Madhya Pradesh, Haryana, Uttar Pradesh, Rajasthan and Bihar, and emerging as the second largest Opposition party in the Lok Sabha after the Swatantra Party.

Thus, the elections brought about a certain balance of forces in the country between the Right and the Left, the North and the South. The Congress still remained the ruling party at the Centre and in eight of the seventeen states. But it was a much-weakened Centre.

Indira's new Cabinet contained much new blood, but it was doubtful whether it would stand up to the stresses and strains of problems, such as the Centre-State Relations, the future of the Fourth Five-Year Plan and the internal divisions within the party. One fact, however, stood out from the elections that India was a democracy and would remain one, in spite of all its troubles.

FIVE

Democracy Still Alive

That secular democracy was still alive and well was also shown by the election of Zakir Husain as India's third President in May 1967. True, then the outgoing President, Sarvepalli Radhakrishnan, India's philosopher and statesman, had to remind politicians in his farewell message that the word 'politician' did not mean 'people of twisted tongues and cold hearts, but those with warm feeling and compassion for the suffering humanity.' But that the heart of the nation was still sound, still capable of looking beyond communal confines to the larger interests of the country was amply demonstrated by Husain's election by a very large majority.

In Husain, India found a President who would rededicate the country to the ideals of Mahatma Gandhi. Speaking immediately after his election, Husain said: 'I shall do my utmost to take our people to what Gandhi strove restlessly to achieve: a pure life, individual and social, an insistence on the means being as pure as the end, an active sympathy for the weak and the downtrodden and a fervent desire to forge unity among the diverse sections of the Indian people as the first condition for helping to establish peace and human brotherhood in the world, based on truth and non violence. This is what he called *'Ram Rajya'*.

Founder and Vice-Chancellor of the Jamia Millia, Zakir Husain had so impressed Gandhiji at the conference on Basic Education (education through a craft) that he had appointed him president of the Hindustan Talim Sangh. After Independence, Husain became Vice-Chancellor of the Aligarh Muslim University. His election as the President of India brought into focus the important place education had in the development of the country. Over 80 per cent of the population was illiterate. Education therefore, he said, in his first broadcast as the President, 'is a prime instrument of national purpose.'

Catholics in India were reminded by Husain's election of the speech he made as vice president at the opening of the International Eucharistic Congress in Bombay. Referring to the influence of the *Bible* on non-Christians, Mahatma Gandhi, he said, was profoundly impressed by the Sermon on the Mount, sought solace in the darkest moments of his life on the teachings of Christ and in his own life gave a shining example of humility and love.

Paying tribute to the Christian contribution to the political, economic and cultural life of the country, Husain referred specially to Kaka Baptista, in whom he said Bombay Catholics could take pride that they had given the country such a remarkable and distinguished personality.

More than Teething Troubles: United Front Falls Apart

Soon after Husain's election, Congress received another setback. The government of D P Mishra lost majority in Madhya Pradesh. The cracks in the monolith had widened. Once again, the cause for the debacle was the division in its own ranks, the infighting and the squabbling for power.

Throwing party loyalty to the winds, distinguished Congressmen crossed the floor andtoppled the government. They were angry that Mishra had dropped three former ministers, favoured the Brahmins and the Mahakoshal region. Three of those rejected had been nominees of the Rajmata of Gwalior. She swore revenge, took advantage of the disaffection, and formed a United Front, The Samyukta Vidhayak Dal, consisting of 110 members, 66 of them Jana Sanghis. Mishra, who was a pillar of the Congress and had snatched Madhya Pradesh from the Jana Sangh, tried his best to bring the defecting Congressmen back but failed and the Samyukta Vidhayak Dal came to power in 1967.

The horse-trading employed was, to say the least, unseemly. Indeed, defection had become a malaise that was ruining the administration. It reduced politics to nothing else but horse-trading that left little time or energy for the task of development.

But defection was a malaise that affected not only the Congress but also the Opposition. One year after the general elections, the euphoria generated by the defeat of the Congress party in a majority of the states and the emergence of the possibility of a two-party system got completely evaporated.

In state after state where the United Front had come into power, the legislatures became dysfunctional and the administration brought to a halt. Over a dozen governments had fallen, 216 legislators had crossed the floor and the President's Rule was imposed on Haryana, West Bengal, Bihar and Uttar Pradesh. With the exception of Madras and Orissa, the rest of the United Front seemed to be Disunited Front, their permutations and combinations making an incredible pattern.

Everywhere, the United Front were cracking up because what brought them together in the first place was only a common opposition to the Congress and a common resolve to keep the Congress out of office. The United Front were a motley collection of parties of the most diverse hues in the political spectrum. Thus, in West Bengal, the rebel Congress which had broken away from the parent body because of its abandonment of Gandhian ideals, tried to get along with the Communists for sometime, but when the Communists came out in their true colours and started inciting peasant revolts and industrial unrest, then a large section of them felt it was time not only to part company with the Communists but also to break away from the rebel Congress party and form a splinter of a splinter.

What specially brought disgrace to democracy in India at this time was the ugly game of floor crossings. In Haryana, it had reached such a dizzy pace and such absurd frequency that it became impossible for any party to show it had a majority in the house for any length of time. In Punjab, 11 legislators crossed the floor several times till finally the defection of 17 members from the United Front brought the government down. In Bihar, three ministries were toppled since the general elections by defections and counter defections from the Congress and the United Front.

The bait of ministership dangled before a prospective defector clearly proved too great a temptation to resist. Ministries had become status symbols, bringing with them emoluments of wealth and power that could turn a pauper into a rich man almost overnight. Whether in the Congress or in the Opposition and at the higher or the lower levels of the administrative machinery, corruption was a fact of life that Indians soon learnt to live with.

SEVEN

Divisive Forces and Gloom

Much of the most dangerous threats to India's democracy and even integrity was the resurgence of the ancient divisive forces of caste and community, language and region. There were too many people who were Hindus or Maharashtrians or Brahmins first. The great mistake made by Jawaharlal Nehru was perhaps the reorganisation of the states on the basis of their language. The result was constant disputes among states about border towns and on what should be the official language. The 'Hindi Down' slogans on the streets of Madras (now Chennai) did not make a person from Uttar Pradesh feel at home in the South. The tearing and burning of English posters in Allahabad or Lucknow made a South Indian feel an alien in these parts, since this was the link language for them.

The emergence of Shiv Sena as a force to be reckoned with in Mumbai Municipal Corporation after the civic elections highlighted the appeal that could be made to regional loyalties and the menace that could be caused by such '*senas*'. These were the armies that made use of strong-arm methods, apart from the normal process of law and order, to protect local or regional interests. The Shiv Sena became synonymous with terror in the minds of the non-Maharashtrians in Mumbai when they went about destroying South Indian restaurants and beating up people who would not vote for them.

Named after Shivaji, the Maratha chieftain who fought against the Mughals from his mountain fortresses in the Western Ghats, the Shiv Sena's main grievance was that in Mumbai, Maharashtrians had a disproportionately small share of the more lucrative jobs that were occupied by South Indians. Similar to the Shiv Sena in Bombay was the Lachit Sena in Assam, which wanted Assam for the Assamese; the Gopal Sena in Kerala, which sought to protect the interests of the Communists. What everybody knew, however, was that these '*senas*' were born and proliferated with the connivance and support of higher-ups in Delhi, who now found that having sown the dragon's teeth, armed men had arisen to devour them.

From Kashmir to Kerala and from Rajasthan to Assam, Hindu religious communalism was raising its ugly head once again. If it was thought that with Partition the ghost of communalism had been laid, the country was in for a rude shock. Communal violence flared up in places as far apart as Calcutta (now Kolkata), Allahabad and Mangalore. Home Minister S B Chavan on one such occasion admitted that it was the Muslims that had the greater number killed in these outbreaks of violence.

With the rise of the Jana Sangh and the Hindu revivalism, the word Hindu began increasingly used synonymously for 'Indian'. Leaflets distributed in Allahabad about this time called upon Hindus in the 'sacred city of Prayag' not to rest till they had driven out every Muslim. Communal riots in Nagpur in June 1968 took a fearful toll of lives. All over the country there seemed to have spread a certain climate of violence, exemplified in the case of a Dalit boy in Andhra Pradesh who was caught stealing slippers of higher caste Hindus. He was tied to a stake and burnt alive while the spectators screamed with delight.

Commenting on Prime Minister Indira Gandhi's statement that what India was suffering from were 'teething troubles', Nirad C Chaudhari, author of the *Continent of Circe* wrote that teething troubles were rather a strange and belated malady to have for a mother with 500 million children and 20 years of domestic autonomy. If the troubles had anything to do with dentition, Nirad Chaudhari continued, they must mean loss of teeth, not their potential appearance.

Certainly, the chorus of ancestral voices prophesying doom for democracy in India had never been greater. It included the voices of Jayaprakash Narayan, at one time considered the only likely successor of Jawaharlal Nehru; Sri Prakasa, former Governor of Bombay; J R D Tata, the well-known industrialist; and a host of others who were not usually given to assuming the role of Cassandras. Vijayalakshmi Pandit, Nehru's sister, resigned as Member Parliament as she felt she was 'out of tune' in Parliament. Certainly, the national mood seemed to be one of one of sullen disgust with the way things were going and apprehension that the chaos and confusion were getting beyond control.

EIGHT

Regionalism and Language

Divisive forces such as regionalism and linguism continued to pose a threat to the unity of the country at the close of the 1960s. In Maharashtra, the Shiv Sena had been agitating for a separate state for Maharashtrians. They now found new grounds for activity in the border dispute between Maharashtra and Mysore, specially over Belgaum, which had a large number of Marathi-speaking people. There was fresh agitation when Morarji Desai visited Bombay (now Mumbai) to present a petition that almost compelled the Centre to bypass the Maha-jan Committee Report and re-open the border issue. Not since Independence had Bombay witnessed such an orgy of violence. Buses, taxis, trains and railway stations went up in flames. Shops were looted and stones pelted at the police when they attempted to control the crowd by means of tear gas.

Curfew was imposed and roads barricaded and it was perhaps only the threat to call in the army that persuaded the Shiv Sainiks to call off the agitation. From his prison cell in Yervada, Bal Thackeray, who had on Republic Day stated that the agitation was aimed at provoking violence and that efforts to check it would be met with violence, sent a message asking the Shiv Sainiks to go to the affected areas to preach peace and put an end to violence. During those four days, 50 people were killed and a thousand arrested.

But it was not only language but also geography and economic considerations that posed a threat to the country's integrity. The process of making language the basis for the reorganisation of states took place first in Andhra Pradesh after the self-immolation of Potishrimalu. It was ironical that the same state now did not see language as enough of a criterion for state formation. Now other factors such as economics and geography were considered more important.

For some time, the people of Telangana had been nursing a grievance that it had not gained appreciably from the creation of Vishala-Andhra and that the agreements for the development of Telangana had not been honoured; funds intended for Telangana had been diverted to the coastal districts and Andhra Pradesh's Chief Minister Brahmananda Reddy was dictatorial and not paying heed to representations.

Students led agitations and three of them burnt themselves. It soon assumed mass dimension when its leadership was taken over by Chenna Reddy to spite the chief minister. The agitators now demanded not just an autonomous sub-state, but a separate state altogether. The chief minister had Chenna Reddy and other leaders arrested and called in the army. Far from quelling the agitation, the arrests only underlined the mass support for the movement and plunged the whole area into greater turmoil and violence than before. Nothing short of a separate Telangana, it appeared, would now satisfy the angry agitators.

On the other hand, the creation of a completely new state, based this time not on linguistic but economic considerations, would have repercussion throughout the country. The danger was that should the claims of Telangana as a separate state be accepted the whole question of states' reorganisation would be in the melting pot again. Other regions like Rayalaseema, Vidharbha and Saurashtra would be staking similar claims for economic reasons and it was hard to see where it would all end.

To add to these problems were the natural disasters such as the floods in Gujarat. Tragedy struck South Gujarat in August 1968 when the waters of Narmada and Tapti rivers swirled in an angry flood over an area of over 2,000 square miles, leaving death and destruction on their wake.

More than 20 inches of rain in 24 hours made it impossible for these rivers to take in the water, which during high tide could not flow into the sea either. Towns, villages, and fields with standing crops were washed away; homes and families drowned; and the survivors reduced to a state of helplessness, disease, hunger and despair. More than 500 people perished and thousands of cattle died. The progress of Gujarat was pushed back by decades. Whatever action the Central and the state governments took proved woefully inadequate.

NINE

Population Control and Poverty Alleviation

In the midst of all the chaos and confusion, Indira Gandhi's government set out to tackle some of the most difficult problems facing the country—population, development and the war against poverty—to which she pledged herself when she took office. Unfortunately, she struck out rather blindly without fully considering the ethical implications of the measures she was adopting.

Population was no doubt the most serious obstacle to the country's development. Its phenomenal increase had, to a large extent, cancelled out the country's economic progress. But the measures undertaken and the lengths to which the government was prepared to go were absurd.

The announcement made by Minister of Health and Family Planning S Chandrasekar that a transistor would be given to every person who underwent a vasectomy had tongues wagging and provided wonderful copy to cartoonists. Later, Chandrasekar's ministry introduced a Bill in Parliament, imposing compulsory sterilisation on all couples having three or more children. Chandrasekar was aware of the moral right of parents to choose the number of children they wanted to have, and had told Parliament that the Bill might be received well and may violate the Constitution. But, at a seminar on family planning, he said that 46 million couples had more than three children and needed to undergo sterilisation. The Maharashtra Government also undertook sterilisation in a big way during 1967. There were in all 1,87,655 sterilisations during the year.

The recourse to such unlawful methods was an abject confession of failure on the part of the country's leaders and an indication that they had thrown up their hands in the struggle for the country's ordered development.

Another reprehensible measure the government undertook in its campaign to control population growth was legalisation, or as the government puts it, the liberalisation of abortion. It was, of course, too much for a country with its traditional and moral moorings to advocate abortion directly as a means to curtail population growth.

Human life is human life and no one, not even the government, has the right to deprive anyone, not even the child in the womb. Because the child in the womb is a human person, any attempt on its life is tantamount to murder. For the state to advocate abortion would therefore be to abdicate one of its basic functions—the preservation of law and order.

In their defence, the government said what they were proposing was not to ask people to abort but to punish abortion as a crime if someone in difficulty resorted to it. But even this proposal could hardly be defended on moral grounds. Murder is murder and always a crime, and it is the duty of the state to prevent it at all cost.

But even to legalise or liberalise abortion in the interest of family planning is to make the child in the womb an unwanted person, someone to be got rid of for all kinds of reasons, social or economic. Legalising abortion cannot be used as a means of family planning or controlling population. This would take the country down the slippery slope that leads to indifference on the part of the people to the sacredness of human life and the decline of morality.

Negative measures, however, were not the only means employed by Indira Gandhi to fight poverty. On 21 April 1969, she placed before Parliament the Drafted Fourth Five-Year Plan with 'Growth with Stability' as its main objective. The hope was that prices would continue to remain stable while the country moved towards self-reliance with less dependence on foreign aid. Some disparities between the very rich and the very poor would continue for some time but an increase in the general development would in the long run benefit everyone and diminish the gap.

A third of India's population still lived below the poverty line, spending Rs 24 per month in urban areas and Rs 15 in rural areas. One-fifth lived below the line of destitution, (Rs 18 in urban and Rs 13 per head in rural areas), clearly the problem of development was the most crucial for the country and the Fourth Plan was meant to address it.

On the other hand, the use of high-yielding varieties of seeds and of fertilisers and insecticides had brought about in many areas in India, especially Punjab, what was called the 'Green Revolution', helped no doubt by two years of good monsoons.

The results of the Fourth Five-Year Plan were estimated to be a five per cent growth in agriculture and an eight to 10 per cent in industry, bringing the total average growth to six per cent per year. Even if these targets were realised by the end of the Plan period, a considerable section of the population would still not be very much above the poverty line.

This Plan envisaged an outlay of Rs 24,400 crore of which about Rs 14,000 crore would be in the public sector. Considering the tremendous requirements of the country, even this amount did not seem too excessive.

As regards agriculture, the Plan provided an aggregate outlay of Rs 2,217 crore in the public sector and estimated a private investment of Rs 1,800 crore. The aim was not only to benefit small farmers to help increase their yield but also to maximise production in areas of promise.

The Fourth Plan sought to extend the frontiers of the Green Revolution and to lessen dependence on the monsoons by an outlay of Rs 1,000 crore on methods of irrigation such as canals, tube wells and pumps. The goal of agricultural development was to achieve self-sufficiency in food and put an end to food imports.

As regards industry, the Plan envisaged an approximate investment of Rs 5,200 crore for organised industry and mining out of which Rs 2,800 crore was for the public sector and Rs 2,400 crore for the private and cooperative sector. The major proportion of outlay in the public sector was for the completion of projects already initiated and projects on which decisions had been taken. New industrial projects were envisaged in high priority fields like fertilisers, petrochemicals and iron ore. All these efforts intented to boost exports and to correct the Balance of Payment (BoP) records.

Transport, urban housing, education, telephones and small scale industries were some of the other areas for development.

The Fourth Five-Year Plan was thus clearly an honest effort to advance the pace of development and fight poverty.

TEN

India's Fourth
Presidential Election

Mid-term elections held in February 1969 in the states of Punjab, Uttar Pradesh, Bihar and West Bengal did not give much promise of stability. They did not provide any reason for the electorate to reject the Congress as it had earlier demonstrated in 1967. Despite disunity in the non-Congress ranks and their poor performance, the electorate by and large still thought that the Congress was no alternative.

In West Bengal, its fortune slumped to a mere 55 in a House of 260 members. The Communist-led United Front won by a thumping majority. No doubt, the Communists had got the support of large sections of the people in West Bengal who looked to them to lift them up from their poverty and misery. Only in Uttar Pradesh did the Congress recover its former prestige and was able to form a government.

In Bihar and Punjab, the picture remained confused. The Jana Sangh too suffered heavy losses, though it had embarked on an ambitious and stridently fanatical programme to increase its strength.

Four months later, in the beginning of May 1969, President Zakir Husain passed away. At a time of crisis when divisive forces threatened the unity of the country, he stood as a symbol of that common heritage and culture that transcended the bonds of caste, community and creed and could speak for the entire nation.

He had gone on an exhausting journey to Assam and returned to Delhi because the strain was too high. He was 'God's good man', as many along the nine-mile route from Rashtrapati Bhavan to the Jamia Milia, uttered. Only a few months earlier he had lit a lamp to inaugurate St John's Medical College in Bangalore.

The death of Zakir Husain and the election of a new President led to another crisis in the Congress party. Never before had a Presidential election been accompanied by so much tension and never before had its outcome been watched with so much trepidation and fear. At any other time, in any other context, a Presidential election might have passed largely unnoticed, since the President's office had been largely ceremonial.

But two years after the 1967 general elections when Congress was defeated in a majority of the states and its majority in Parliament drastically reduced, and three years before the 1972 general elections, when, even according to the most optimistic forecasts, Congress could hope to come to power only in coalition with other parties, a Presidential election was fraught with great consequences, since when no single party has the majority, it is up to the President to decide which party leader to approach to form a government.

Add to this was the fact that the fighting within the Congress ranks, aggravated by the Syndicate, consisting mostly of conservative old men, who chose Neelam Sanjiva Reddy as official Congress candidate for Presidential election, reached such a stage when the party seemed to be in danger of splitting right and left.

Indira returned to India after a triumphant tour of Japan and Indonesia only to find herself faced with a Presidential candidate whom she would find hard to get on with, if ever he was elected.

What upset Indira the most was that she saw in the snap vote a clever move to edge her out of the premiership or at least to undermine her influence in the party.

Her fears were not entirely groundless. It was a known fact that among the higher echelons of the party there had been a constant jockeying for power ever since the death of Jawaharlal Nehru.

Indira had become prime minister because she happened to be a compromise candidate, least objectionable to all. But, she succeeded in keeping her place by playing one against another, and in the meanwhile, by projecting an image of the prime minister as the real leader of the country.

The fact that she was Nehru's daughter helped her considerably in the process. Having been out-manoeuvred so often, the Syndicate naturally got together, whilst she was away, and thought to get the better of her by agreeing on the choice of a candidate who would put her in her place when he became President.

All that happened afterwards—her sacking of Morarji Desai as finance minister, the hasty nationalisation of the banks, however justified or unjustified it might have been on its own merits, her demand for a free vote that in reality meant asking Congress members to vote for Varahagiri Venkata Giri—all that was only understandable in the light of Indira trying to secure her position as prime minister.

Doubtless ideological reasons were mixed up with personal ones for most of these actions, but it was extremely unlikely that Indira would have pushed them through had she not been fighting for her own political survival.

At the end of the day, there was no split in the Congress party, at least not just yet. After nearly two months of bitter squabbling and abusive name-calling that threatened to split the Congress organisation down the middle and to plunge the country into one of its most severe crises since Independence, the leaders of the warring factions got together, five days after the election of V V Giri as India's fourth president and decided to bury the hatchet.

After all the anathemas hurled against Indira and her supporters, and after all the threats of action against them for defying party discipline, the final resolution passed by the Congress Working Committee came almost as an anti-climax. All it did to mollify the party organisation men, the Syndicate, who now retired sullenly into their tents to lick their wounds, was to admit that 'mistakes had been made by both sides.'

But it adamantly refused to censure the prime minister and her followers for having supported Giri against the official Congress candidate Sanjiva Reddy.

In fact, the election of Giri, more than being a victory for Giri, was a personal triumph for Indira Gandhi.

That in the count of the first preference votes Giri should have led by over 87,000 votes and secured a majority in 11 out of the 17 states of the Indian Union, in spite of Sanjiva Reddy being the official Congress candidate, was a clear proof that the caucus of party bosses, led by Congress president Nijalingappa, did not command any sizable following even in the ranks of the party itself.

Once the election results were declared, the Syndicate knew it had lost its hold on the levers of power, both in the party and in the country. The net result, therefore, of the tumultuous events of those two months was the emergence of Indira Gandhi as the real leader of the country, with her hands considerably strengthened by the election of Giri as the President of India.

Already, her socialist measures had won for her, rightly or wrongly, a certain amount of popular acclaim.

The nationalisation of the banks may have been a move in the game of political chess, but it was also meant to boost the sagging fortune of the Congress by making a greater amount of credit available to the small industrialists and the peasant farmer who had not shared in the profits of the green revolution. The prophets of doom could still be proved wrong about the 1972 elections.

ELEVEN

The Split in the Congress

Though an imminent split in the Congress party was averted, the struggle between the two rival groups was far from over. The power of the party bosses had not been definitively broken. In at least three states—Gujarat, Mysore and Uttar Pradesh, the Presidential election showed, the Syndicate still commanded the allegiance of the chief ministers and the majority of Congressmen. Men like Ashoka Mehta, Ram Subhag Singh and Sadiq Ali had also joined them.

There was a scramble to seize the property of the parent body for one side or the other and the merry game of defection from one group to another went on. Both the sides had burnt their bridges and had little desire for unity. It became clear from the fact that the two groups decided to have separate plenary sessions, one in Bombay and the other in Ahmedabad. Congressmen were asked to go to one or the other, to stand up and be counted.

Huge crowds attended the Ahmedabad session. Clearly, the Opposition Congress could not be dismissed as a mere splinter group, run by old cronies who already had passed their prime. On the other hand, still larger crowds turned up in Bombay to welcome Jagjivan Ram and attend the New Congress Plenum, showing clearly that it had the majority of Congressmen in its fold. Neither party could claim to be the rightful successor of the parent Congress. But the lines were now clearly drawn. The split was confirmed and sealed.

At the Ahmedabad session, the Opposition Congress attacked Indira Gandhi for aligning with the Communists. They rejected nationalisation of the export-import trade, of general insurance and of wholesale trade in food grains. They wanted the abolition of the princes' privy purses to be gradual.

The New Congress, headed by Indira Gandhi , was fully committed to the early abolition of these relics of colonialism and the nationalisation of general insurance. They worked for procurement of cereals by the state and a dominant role for it in export trade, but refrained from any timetable for a ceiling on property. The Opposition Congress appeared slightly right of centre and the ruling Congress slightly left.

In the early 1970s, Indian politics appeared increasingly strange. It came to be realised that the quarrel that had led to the split in the Congress was not really of ideology but of personalities. The old Congress had a hard core of right inclined leadership and the new Congress an equally hard-core of Leftist Young Turks. But a fairly large membership in both the parties was uncommitted one way or the other.

Indeed, ideology had become such an irrelevant issue that the New Congress was prepared to do business with the Swatantra Party in Gujarat to topple the old Congress ministry of Hitendra Desai and the Swatantra Party was also prepared to do business with the New Congress for the same purpose, though its avowed aim was to topple the Indira government at the Centre.

Though as a result of the nationalisation of banks, Indira Gandhi had come to be immensely popular and remained head and shoulders above the other national figures, much of her time and energy were spent in the struggle for survival. She could not give the country the leadership it needed for development. Nor was there any strengthening of the organisational side of the New Congress. In the Rajya Sabha elections, many of the New Congress supporters in Orissa, Maharashtra and other states voted for others, thus causing a split within the split.

TWELVE

India After the Split

The record of New Congress rule in India after the split was not altogether dismal. The creation of the state of Meghalaya in the Garo and Mizo hills of Assam (for a long time the scene of much tribal unrest) and the settlement of the question whether Chandigarh, the city built by Le Corbusier, should belong to Punjab or Haryana were solid achievements that would have done credit to any government.

Some of the credit for the easing of the food situation and the more favourable balance of trade went to the government. But by and large it could be said that the struggle for survival had prevented Indira from getting on with the job and pursuing the kind of dynamic policy that would have checked the growth of unemployment and the rise in prices and stilled the unrest and discontent prevailing among the landless peasants in the countryside.

The confusion was not limited to the New Congress alone. The elderly in the old Congress, such as Morarji Desai and Nijalingappa, having been cast out into the political wilderness, were consoling themselves with hurling abuses at Indira Gandhi. The party failed to come out with any constructive proposal or an alternative policy. The Swatantra Party, the party of free enterprise, was determined to overthrow Indira government but ganged up with her party in Gujarat.

A party that was not confused but was the cause for much confusion and division in the country was the Jana Sangh. Inspired by the dream of the Rashtriya Swayamsewak Sangh, the Jana Sangh kept on beating the drums of communal hatred and fanning the fires of communal passion. Its current thesis was that Muslims, Christians and other minorities were not in the 'mainstream' of Indian life and culture and should, therefore, be Indianised—that is Hinduised. The Muslims too had their fanatics and the direct result of such talk were the frequent outbreaks of communal violence that left only bitterness and destruction of life and property in their wake.

In May 1970, in Bhiwandi, thirty miles from Bombay, Hindus and Muslims killed each other in hundreds and indulged in an orgy of looting, arson and rape. This occurred after a mammoth procession, held to commemorate the birthday of Shivaji, the Maratha chieftain, who had fought the Mughals and whose cult was being fostered by the Shiv Sena. Still another source of confusion, division and disorder in the country were the communists. There were three varieties: The Moscow-oriented Communist Party of India (CPI), the Peking-oriented Communist Party of India-Marxist (CPM) and the Naxalites who believed in changing social and economic order through violent revolution.

The CPM-led United Front governments in Kerala and West Bengal were both toppled and President's rule imposed. In Kerala, the United Front cracked up because some of its members were charged with corruption. The state had a mid-term poll on 17 September 1970, which resulted in the victory of the new Congress-led Leftist alliance largely due to Indira Gandhi's personal campaigning.

But in West Bengal, the Marxists plunged the state into such an orgy of misrule that there was a complete breakdown of law and order. To win over the mass of workers they incited them to strike or *gherao* their employers and then used the police to shield the lawbreakers. Six hundred murders and nine hundred atrocities in eleven months was the terrible record of Marxist Jyoti Basu's Home Ministry.

The result was that industries pulled out of West Bengal causing widespread unemployment and ultimately the government collapsed. The breakdown of law and order, however, continued in West Bengal. Almost everyday some atrocity was being perpetrated by the Naxalites, who derived their name from Naxalbari where they first started operations; they were inciting the landless peasantry to grab the 'surplus' lands of the rich landlords.

It was to draw the reins of power into her hands that Indira Gandhi carried out her Cabinet reshuffle. In the process, by taking over the important Home Ministry from Y B Chavan and four other portfolios from others and transferring them to less important offices, she sidelined her rivals. These moves, however, alarmed her adversaries, who began accusing her of being a dictator, of exploiting the fears of the minorities for her own purposes, of getting her priorities wrong in making out communalism a greater danger than Communism, of being soft on the Indian Communists and condoning their atrocities and of selling the country's foreign policy to the Russians. Meeting in Delhi, the Old Congress sent out a call for a grand alliance of all the 'nationalist democratic and socialist forces' in the country.

How an alliance, grand or not-so-grand, could bring such mutually opposed parties as the old Congress, the Swatantra Party, the Jana Sangh, the SSP (Samyukta Socialist Party) and even the Peking Communists into one group was unclear to all except the party rhetoricians, who had but one idea in their minds: how to topple Indira Gandhi. In the event, the alliance almost proved to be a non-starter. The Rightist parties found it impossible to come together with the Leftists and among the Rightists themselves the old Congress members and the Swatantra Party members in Gujarat refused to have anything to do with each other, in spite of the directives of the central executives of both parties. Finally, the whole idea seemed to have come to an ignoble end when a no-confidence motion in Parliament against Indira Gandhi lost by nearly a hundred votes.

But barely had the government ridden out the storm of the Grand Alliance when it was faced with another crisis. In a vain bid to out-do the Naxalites, the Leftist parties launched a country-wide movement to grab the land of the rich landlords and of the government. True, there were many social injustices crying out to be corrected and the land reform acts had so many loopholes that they could be easily circumvented.

But that the land-grab movement was no more than a gimmick to draw the votes of the peasant masses was clear from the fact that the leaders spoke in so many voices about the real purpose of the movement and had no clear idea about whose lands were to be grabbed or how they were to be distributed.

Moreover, such a movement was an open defiance of law and order and an incitement to violence on a mass scale. Fortunately, the movement fizzled out without much violence, having achieved little or nothing beyond getting 8,500 land grabbers clapped into jail.

Emboldened by the vote of confidence and probably under pressure from the Left, the prime minister introduced the Princes' Privy Purses Abolition Bill in 1971–72 in the Parliament.

The amount doled out annually to the princes was negligible, but it was argued that after twenty-three years of Independence, the princes had become an anachronism and that a Socialist state should not feel bound to any feudal obligations entered into by the colonial rulers even if these were enshrined in the Constitution.

The Bill secured the two-thirds majority in the Lower House but failed to obtain it in the Upper House by just one vote. Whereupon, the President of India passed an order that 'derecognised' the princes. A whole era in history was thus sought to be brought to a close by the President's fiat. But the era was not as yet closed since the Supreme Court found the President's order unconstitutional.

THIRTEEN

Indira gets Mandate

Though Indira Gandhi declared that the calling of general elections 14 months ahead of the schedule was no gamble at all, there must have been some calculated risk involved. After all, Opposition governments were in power in a majority of the Indian states.

But Indira had sensed the mood of the people and was confident that if she went to them and asked for a mandate for herself and her party, they would most willingly give it to her. The elections in Kerala had demonstrated very clearly that her popularity with the masses was immense and that the personal triumph that she had scored on that occasion could be repeated on a much grander scale in the national election.

Tired of the ceaseless struggle for political survival she was waging, frustrated in her bid to put an end to the violence in West Bengal and other parts of the country, balked at every turn by vested interests in her attempts to bring a new deal to her people, Indira decided to strike while the iron was still hot.

Whatever other motives, her adversaries might have imputed to her for calling the elections so early, the fact was that once the split in the Congress had occurred, Indira's party was reduced to the status of a minority government dependent upon the support of the Leftist and regional parties. Hence, a mid-term poll seemed to be necessary sooner rather than later. Had she waited till 1972, the general elections would have coincided with the state assembly elections, and national issues would have been obscured by local and regional problems.

From the word 'go', Indira Gandhi never looked back. Boarding a small plane, she hopped from city to city and state to state, covering in her whirlwind tour almost the entire length and breadth of the country, including such states as Mysore, Gujarat and West Bengal, where Opposition governments were in power. Although on one occasion, she had sandals flung at her from the audience, the reception she received in general was so tremendous and enthusiastic that it was evident she had stepped into her father's shoes as the darling of the masses.

Caught on the wrong foot, even when they had sufficient warning of a mid-term poll in the offing, her rivals went about frantically trying to form a 'grander alliance' with whomsoever they could. How this motley collection of parties—the old Congress, the Jana Sangh, the Swatantra Party, the Samyukta Socialist Party (SSP), the Shiv Sena and the Bharatiya Kranti Dal (BKD)—could ever come together in the first place, passed all understanding.

Revelling in paradoxes, this monstrous Caliban seemed to assume the most unnatural shapes. It did not seem to mind that the SSP was for abolishing the very Right to Property while the Jana Sangh clung to property considering it to be as dear as life. The SSP wanted a new Constituent Assembly to frame a brand new constitution to usher in a Socialist Utopia, while the Swatantra

Party and the old Congress would countenance no such move; that the Jana Sangh wanted to 'Indianise' those Indians whom they thought not sufficiently Indian since they did not belong to the Hindu religion, while the Swatantra Party and the old Congress promised solemnly they would uphold all the rights of minorities such as the Muslims and the Christians. The Swatantra Party forgot its own identity so much that it did not mention the term 'free enterprise' in its manifesto, while the old Congress forgot its socialism so much that it emerged as a party of the Right.

Despite their efforts, the Grand Alliance could not reach a common minimum programme or sketch a policy that would provide an alternative viable government. All that they could boast of having in common was a shared hatred for Indira Gandhi, who they said was a dictator out to sell the country to the Russians and bring in Communism through the back door, corrupting the morals of public life and using power for her own selfish purposes. 'Indira must go' was their war cry.

In striking contrast, Indira Gandhi did not answer insults with insult or abuse with abuse. The war she waged was not against the Grand Alliance but against poverty. Her approach was positive, not negative. 'Poverty must go, disparity must diminish, injustice must end' — such was the rallying call of the New Congress manifesto.

The message she delivered to the millions throughout the country was that a crash programme of public construction projects would be launched so as to bring down the level of unemployment, that the small farmer would be able to take part in the green revolution by having credit and other facilities made available to him, that large-scale housing programmes for the middle income groups and slum clearance would be undertaken, that small industry would be the growth point and that regulations would be simplified and delays avoided.

Indira Gandhi's New Congress manifesto disabused the minds of those who felt that she wanted to abolish private property or stifle private enterprise by declaring that the Right to Property would remain and that as many as possible should be able to enjoy it.

Disparities, of course, would have to diminish. Hence, individual land holdings and ownership of urban property would not be allowed to exceed reasonable limits. General insurance would be taken over and state participation in the export and import trade would be increased. Constitutional difficulties in carrying through some of these measures would be overcome by changes or amendments in the Constitution. Thus, the government would steer clear both of 'Right Reaction' and 'Left Adventurism'. It would be socialist and moderately radical, Left of Centre but not too far Left.

The whirligig of time brings its own revenges. When Indira Gandhi was chosen prime minister after the death of Lal Bahadur Shastri, the old guard that constituted the Congress leadership thought that she would be a pawn in the game while they fought it out among themselves. They scarcely expected Indira Gandhi to start asserting herself and when she did so, as on the question of the nationalisation of the banks and the Presidential election, a crisis was precipitated that led to the split in the Congress.

The crusty elderly were now firmly and finally humbled and Indira Gandhi emerged from the elections as the sole and undisputed leader of the party and country. The 'Grand Alliance' of which the Old Guards were the chief architects collapsed due to its own inherent contradictions.

All the rhetoric about acting 'before the lights of liberty are finally dimmed' proved empty. Between themselves the Grand Alliance parties could not win even 50 seats, as against the 350 of the New Congress. Most of the old Congress leaders, like S K Patil, Nijalingappa, Ram Subhag Singh and Ashoka Mehta, were sent into the wilderness. Mysore wholly and Gujarat half lost to the New Congress. It was doubtful if the old Congress had any other option but to fold up or return to the New Congress. For that matter it was doubtful if the Swatantra Party or the SSP had any future in the political scenario.

Indira Gandhi had the mandate she wanted—and very much more. She did not have to look over her shoulder now to see how the Communists or anybody else were taking any of her proposed measures. Difficulties from the Constitution would not prove insuperable as she had the two-thirds majority necessary for making changes in it. But therein precisely lay the challenge she was called upon to face. As long as she was leading a minority government she had the excuse that if the country was falling behind on the road to progress, it was because of the opposition or vested interests or the Constitution. Now the government would be judged by its own actual performance.

Nor would the people who had voted for her make any allowances. Their mood as in 1967 was still an angry one. In 1967, they were angry and disenchanted with the Congress because all it had to show for over fifteen years of undisputed rule was corruption, inefficiency and bureaucracy. So, they humbled the great Congress monolith and made it share its power with a spectrum of political parties, ranging from extreme Right to extreme Left. This time they were angry with the politicians who had made politics a dirty game of toppling and defections and formed coalitions that had come to grief almost as soon as they had been formed. They were angry at the scale of lawlessness, divisiveness and instability that plagued the country and were afraid that a coalition government at the Centre might well be the beginning of the end.

Giving so much power to one person and one party and depriving Parliament of any opposition worth the name might not in the long term seem to be good for democracy in India, but it was the only option left with the people if they wanted change with stability.

In Indira, they found their symbol of hope and gave her the mandate she wanted. The patience of the Indian people was proverbial but even this could wear thin and if Indira were to prove unable to deliver the goods and redeem the promises she had made, their anger might well be visited on her when the time came.

Indira Gandhi was fully alive to the tremendous challenge that her mandate presented. When unruffled and in command of the situation, she had shown the capacity for the kind of responsible action that leads to true progress. So she would not be rushed by some of her exuberant colleagues into courses of action that would mean, 'levelling down' without at the same time 'levelling up'.

FOURTEEN

The Unmaking of Pakistan

The general elections of 1971 swept Indira Gandhi to an over-whelming victory. It was ironical that just when India seemed to be entering a period of stability and progress, Pakistan went in for a major crisis. The same democratic process led to the dismember-ment and unmaking of Pakistan.

Had Pakistan's short-lived experiment in democracy succeeded, the country would have had a federate or confederate constitution and Sheikh Mujib-ur Rehman, as Pakistan's President Yahya Khan said, would have been its first Prime Minister. In the elections of December 1970, the Sheikh's Awami League captured 167 of the 169 National Assembly seats allotted to East Pakistan while Zulfiqar Ali Bhutto's People Party got only 88 of the 144 seats reserved for West Pakistan.

The Sheikh and his Awami League, therefore, had the near unanimous support of the 75 million people of East Bengal whilst

Bhutto and his People's Party had only just over half of the 58 million people of West Pakistan behind them. By all democratic standards, therefore, the Sheikh and his Awami League rather than Bhutto and his People's Party were the true representatives of the majority of the people of Pakistan. But the tragedy of Pakistan was that the minority was determined to lord it over the majority, even if it meant that Pakistan's experiment in democracy would be aborted. The elections had been held to prepare for a National Assembly that would hammer out a constitution for the country and 3 March 1971 had been fixed for the convening of the Constituent Assembly. But suddenly Yahya Khan announced that the date had been postponed. East Pakistan suspected that the postponement was due to the manoeuvres of Bhutto whom the president had consulted while he chose to bypass the Sheikh. Violence erupted and lasted for five days.

Yahya Khan asked Sheikh and Bhutto to meet informally on 10 March 1971 to thrash out their differences. Sheikh refused and the President was forced to announce the convening of the Assembly on 25 March. Meanwhile, both the President and Bhutto came to Dacca for talks with the Sheikh who stipulated as his conditions for attending the National Assembly that martial law be ended; the troops return to their barracks; enquiries be made into the shootings of the previous week; and civilian rule be installed by transferring power to the elected representatives of the people. At the same time, the Sheikh ordered a general strike.

President Yahya Khan had apparently agreed to Sheikh's four conditions and a compromise seemed to have been reached. But as soon as the President left East Pakistan, the army let loose a reign of terror in which 85 people died and more than 200 were injured. Before Bhutto left, Dacca had gone up in flames.

Sheikh Mujib-ur Rehman went on air to broadcast his Declaration of Independence over the 'Voice of Independent Bangladesh.'

He was promptly arrested, charged with treason and put into prison. From then on, Pakistan was torn apart. There were two nations now, one fighting for the independence of Bangladesh and the other attempting to crush it. What happened in East Pakistan was the mass upsurge of an entire people determined to take their destiny into their own hands against the armed might of an oppressive regime. From then on the existence of two separate nations was a settled and historic fact, whatever the technical or judicial position and whichever way the fortunes of war turned.

Unlike the pro-Peking Maulana Bhashani, who had been agitating for complete independence, Sheikh Mujib-ur Rehman never wanted a complete dismemberment of the two wings of Pakistan. What he wanted was provincial autonomy, with the central government keeping control of defence, currency and foreign affairs. But even this proved unacceptable to the people of West Pakistan, who felt their dominant hold over the entire country threatened.

Provincial autonomy, however, was the least that could have satisfied the people of East Pakistan. When Pakistan was carved out from the former British Indian Empire, it was thought that religion would be a binding factor between the two wings of Pakistan, separated though they were by 1,200 miles of Indian territory. But religion alone had not been able to erase the deep-seated differences between two distinct peoples, one of which boasted of its close links with the Middle East and took pride in the Urdu language, with its close affinities with Persian and Arabic, while the other gloried in the Bengali language and culture and loved to sing the songs of Rabindranath Tagore.

The attempt to foist Urdu on East Pakistan and to make it the sole official language of Pakistan was resisted at a very early stage in the country's history, but the hatred aroused by that attempt had increased and simmered with the passage of time because of the continuous exploitation of the East by the West.

The personnel of the army and the civil services were heavily drawn from the West and every time there was trouble in East Bengal which became East Pakistan, it was the soldiers from West Pakistan who were sent to suppress it. By its sale of jute and other raw materials, East Pakistan was earning half of Pakistan's foreign exchange, yet in return it received a mere 30 per cent of the government's annual budget. Raw jute was produced in the East but sent to the West to be processed. The twenty-five giant industrial projects, the three big fertiliser factories, the sugar mills and the cement factories were all located in the West whilst even such industries as existed in the East were in the hands of West Pakistani businessmen. It was no wonder that the per capita income of the West was 37.9 per cent higher than in the East; that the West's rate of growth was 6.9 per cent as against the East's 2.6 per cent; that almost a third of the people in East Bengal were unemployed and that the rest just managed to exist.

Mohammed Ali Jinnah's dream of Muslims as one nation now lay shattered on the paddy fields of Bangladesh, where Muslims spilt the blood of Muslims. Religion alone had proved to be an insufficient basis for a country's nationalism. On 25 March 1971, the Pakistani army cracked down on East Bengal and proceeded to carry out genocide, the enormity of which was unequalled in recent times. Pakistan's experiment in democracy was cruelly and finally aborted. President Yahya Khan attempted, in a broadcast, to show that he wanted to put new life into it but could deceive nobody, least of all international opinion. They were horrified by the unlimited wickedness of the crimes that continued to perpetrate in East Bengal.

India was in a difficult position. It could not be insensitive to the sufferings, and killings in East Bengal. But it did not want to do anything that would imply it was making capital out of Pakistan's troubles for her its own interests. Even so, Pakistan twice accused India of interfering in its internal affairs. On 31 March 1971, both houses of Parliament felt it was time to speak out and voice 'the whole-hearted support of the people of India' for the 'struggle and sacrifices' of the people of Bangladesh. Prime Minister Indira Gandhi read the declaration expressing 'deep anguish and grave concern' at the developments in Bangladesh and calling upon all governments to prevail upon the Pakistani government to 'put an end immediately to the systematic decimation of a people, which amounts to genocide.'

With the coming of the monsoon, the first stage of the war ended and the second began. The brave but disorganised freedom fighters of Bangladesh known as the *Mukti Fauz* (Liberation Army) realised that an open confrontation with the highly organised and well-armed West Pakistan army was not possible. Only a long continued harassment of the enemy would bring them victory.

In such a guerilla type of warfare the disadvantages would be with the West Pakistan army, whose men would be operating in hostile territory. They would have to stick to the roads whilst the guerillas would be moving about freely. They were on home ground and knew the marshy terrain with its many streams and rivulets.

Even so, the outcome was not immediately predictable. The West Pakistanis had Chinese tacticians to guide them and had secured landing craft and assault boats from Turkey. What the guerillas lacked was an organised and united command to coordinate their activities. The danger was that the leadership of the liberation forces might slip to Communist and Maoist elements that were well versed in guerilla warfare. The Awami League leaders had formed a provisional Government of Bangladesh with Nazrul

Islam as acting President and Tajuddin Ahmed as Prime Minister. They were good debaters but not good soldiers.

The first stage of the war ended with the West Pakistan army gaining control of the larger towns and cities, like Dacca, Chittagong and Jessore, whilst the freedom fighters seemed to have a strong base in the countryside. Fighting with stones, bamboo staves, knives and spears, bows and arrows and rifles of the Second World War vintage, the freedom fighters were no match for the vastly superior West Pakistan forces. The air force swung into action, bombing cities and towns and whose infantry, artillery and American M-24 tanks decimated whole sections of unarmed civilian populations. In Dacca alone 7,000 people were reported to have perished, their bodies floated in the river almost as 'thick as autumnal leaves that strew the brooks in Vallombrosa.' The liberation forces claimed they had killed an estimated 1,000 West Pakistani troops, but against this the civilian and army losses of East Bengal were estimated at more than four lakh.

The terrible killing or genocide, as Sheikh Mujib-ur Rehman called it, has been well documented by independent foreign journalists, who were ordered to leave East Pakistan shortly after the fighting broke out. The very fact that West Pakistan refused to allow Red Cross volunteers to enter East Bengal seemed to confirm the enormity of the scale of the genocide.

FIFTEEN

The Great Exodus

The authorities in West Pakistan tried to make out that all was calm and quiet but could not hide the truth that the tide of refugees from East Bengal had risen to a flood. Across the 1,349-mile frontier with India, they came pouring into Assam or Tripura or West Bengal, leaving all behind and expecting very little but bringing with them a thousand tragic tales of savagery and brutality. Over four lakh of them were registered in May with the Government of India, but the total number easily passed the million mark. Every available empty space, school or cattle shed or railway platform was being made use of to provide some shelter for these hapless victims, some of whom had seen their entire families lined up against the wall and shot one by one.

By the end of October 1971, two to three million had fled from Pakistan to India, in what Pope Paul VI called 'one of the most dramatic movements of population known to human history.'

Till the end of March 1971, Agartala, for instance, was a quiet little provincial town, lost in a long valley among the hills of Tripura. Then suddenly in April the idyll was destroyed and Agartala's peace shattered. From across the nearby Indo-Pakistani border hundreds of thousands of refugees poured into the sleepy town, trying to find whatever shelter they could. Those who had money rented vacant rooms, others stayed with friends and relatives, and still others made their homes in classrooms or temple compounds or under the branches of trees. From 1.6 million, Tripura's population shot up to 3 million. Guns started booming across the border and the continuous shelling shook and rattled the windowpanes of the houses in the town. Stray bullets landed in the Government Secretariat building, killing and wounding a few people.

Panic seized Agartala. Most ghastly sight of all, *Mukti Fauz* soldiers, their blood spilling from their gaping wounds, struggled to reach Agartala's hospitals in such large numbers that the doctors and nurses found themselves hopelessly unequal to the task. But the government and the people of Agartala rose manfully to the occasion. Under the leadership of then Lt Governor A L Dias, Agartala began humming with activity. Slowly but surely out of the confusion and chaos an efficient organisation arose. On the slopes of the hills or on the raised ground of the rolling country around Agartala, neat, trim refugee camps, with hutments made of reed and thatch and patterned after the houses in the villages of Tripura, gave hundreds of thousands of homeless refugees some sort of a home away from home.

Elsewhere, along the more than thousand-mile-long border, conditions in the refugee camps were not always so satisfactory. There was the Salt Lake City Refugee Camp, for example, that lay south of Calcutta's Dum Dum airport and harboured some two lakh people. Its hutments extended row upon row for nearly three miles. Standing at one end one could hardly see the other. The government built these simple hutments out of palm leaf strips with a bamboo framework and polythene roofing. Each family was allotted a space of 5 ft by 8 ft marked off only by a thin jute cord. There in that narrow space of uneven ground, men, women and children ate, drank, cooked and slept, while the heavy monsoon rains beat in, turning the mud into slush and the slush into puddles of mucky water.

Outside, in the so-called passageways between the hutments, ran the open gutters carrying the stench of defecation, although mercifully sprayed with insecticides. And everywhere there were bodies—bodies of naked children with protruding stomachs and ribs sticking out; bodies of half-naked men and women, clad in dirty, unwashed clothes; thin, dark weary, emaciated bodies swarming around the water taps; or squatting in the slush in thousands, waiting from 4 o'clock in the morning, waiting for the distribution of bread or milk powder or rations to begin. For the most part these were idle bodies, doing no work, because doing work would have brought the price of Calcutta labour down.

All this led to an air of listlessness, frustration and despair. True, there was no actual starvation, not many deaths from hunger. The government provided 400 grams of rice and 300 grams of pulses on each ration card and the Caritas India distributed daily 20,000 loaves of sweet vitaminised bread, donated by the US Catholic Relief Services. This was just about enough to keep body and soul together, but not enough to restore the energies drained by the long trek from East Pakistan. There were the sick bodies resulting from malnutrition, crowding around the dispensary; they waited to be examined by the Holy Cross doctors or lying in the pneumonia, typhoid, dysentery and gastroenteritis wards being looked after by the nuns of Mother Teresa or some other congregation.

There were also the dead bodies wrapped in plastic and piled up in a tent called the morgue. They waited to be disposed off by burial or cremation. Sometimes the wait was too long; they started to stink. One passed the tent with a shudder. A corpse could be lying across the entrance, hardly visible through the plastic.

One reason why conditions in Salt Lake City were so miserable—the camp was unwieldy. Other camps like the one on Calcutta-Petropole Road were smaller and, therefore, more manageable. Yet, even they were not in the best of condition; some lay in knee-deep water. The crowded transit camps where fresh arrivals went to register themselves were scenes of appalling human misery. There was the sheer magnitude of numbers.

Not only were there scores of camps on both sides of the road but also as you approached the border the road itself was lined with huts on both sides for a full stretch of fifteen miles. The Indian government did its best. Voluntary agencies helped—Catholic-aid agencies particularly like Caritas, CRS, Misereor, Secours Catholique and CAFOD. But the problem was so gigantic that it almost defied solution. By mid-October, 40 thousand were still coming in every day and the total was expected to reach 12 million by the end of 1971.

Each of these eight million refugees had his own story to tell and in every one of these stories the elements were the same: the burning and the looting, the raping and the killing by the West Pakistan soldiers, the leaving of home and property, the taking of the long road with its innumerable hazards to the border or the travelling by boat on turbulent rivers, and then the dash to freedom under cover of night and the thick jungle bushes.

At the border, there was always the risk of being fired upon, but refugees who had gone before sent word to their friends and relatives on the best escape routes and so the exodus continued. Some were fortunate that they could come with their whole families. But all too often husbands had been separated from their wives, fathers from their sons and mothers from their daughters and they did know one another's whereabouts. Occasionally, news came from Bangladesh that a husband had been shot, a sister raped and killed and then there was the agony repeated in all its horror.

SIXTEEN

The Liberation Army

It was not only refugees who came through the border. In Agartala strapping young men, wearing *lungis* (sarongs), could be seen marching four abreast down the road. They were the *Mukti Fauz* (Liberation Army) men, now called the *Mukti Vahini*.

When the trouble first started, so many wounded *Mukti Fauz* soldiers came through the border that there was no place for them even in the corridors of the hospitals. In late October, there were still two wards that were filled with them and whenever there was a guerilla raid nearby some more were sure to arrive. Some had their limbs mangled, some their hands or legs amputated, some carried bullet wounds on their bodies. But all of them bore such a hatred for the Pakistanis that, whatever happened, they would go back and fight once they had recovered.

The *Mukti Vahini* volunteers who came through the border, asked for asylum and the Indian government accordingly gave them food and shelter. The *Mukti Vahini* commanders took them in, giving them physical and later military training. When they were ready they were sent back to Bangladesh to fight alongside other guerillas, some of whom might have been trained locally. There they used their hit-and-run tactics, blew up bridges, disrupted communications, made guerilla raids or units of the Pakistani army and in general harassed the Pakistani authorities. They were now in control of several areas inside Bangladesh.

Since these guerillas were natives of the place, they could set out on their forays and return to their villages to merge again into the local population without the Pakistani authorities being any the wiser. The strength of the *Mukti Vahini* was put at about 25,000. In comparison, the Pakistani army had 1,20,000 men equipped with Chinese and American arms.

But what the *Mukti Vahini* people said was that every able-bodied man in Bangladesh was a potential *Mukti Vahini* soldier and would fight as such in the hour of need. Conditions inside Bangladesh, said the *Mukti Vahini*, were far from normal. Industry and commerce were at a standstill. Jute mills had closed down and only a skeleton staff attended this municipal and government offices. The Pakistan army was plundering the crops in an attempt to create an artificial famine and drive still greater numbers into India. Given Independence Bangladesh could easily become an entirely viable nation.

That the *Mukti Vahini* was being aided and abetted by India was, as *Time* magazine said, not even denied by India. Why should it have been? After all, India had eight million refugees on her hands and the cost of supporting them was weakening her already shaky economy. What had India done to be asked to bear such an insupportable burden? How long could her patience be tried?

So long as the military *Junta* in Islamabad refused to come to terms with the *Mukti Vahini* and so long as Sheikh Mujib-ur Rehman languished in prison and awaited a trial with a foregone conclusion, there was not the remotest prospect of normal conditions returning to East Bengal or of the eight million refugees returning to their homes.

The *Mukti Vahini* were now in no mood whatsoever for any political solution short of complete independence. After the genocide and continued repression by the army, there could be no compromise.

Equally clearly, a war between India and Pakistan would benefit nobody, least of all the *Mukti Vahini*. Such a war would lead to the globalisation of the conflict and in that situation Bangladesh would be largely forgotten.

At the beginning of August 1971, there were rumours that India would officially recognise Bangladesh on 15 August—the day of her own independence. That would of course, imply that Bangladesh could then officially ask for aid from India and India would officially give it to her, thereby provoking Pakistan to declare war on India.

Fortunately, Indira Gandhi showed considerable restraint and nothing of the kind happened. Instead India and the Soviet Union signed a treaty, promising that they would help each other to avert any threat of aggression against either of them.

What the *Mukti Vahini* said was: 'Leave it to us to fight it out and we will wear the enemy down till, out of sheer exasperation, Pakistan agrees to the independence of Bangladesh. Bangladesh may struggle to be born for months, perhaps for years, but please God someday it shall.'

SEVENTEEN

The Birth of Bangladesh

Pakistan refused to even admit the existence of *Mukti Vahini*. It talked only of repelling the attacks of 'Indian infiltrators' and threatened a war against India. Indira Gandhi showed considerable restraint and refused to be hustled into a course of action that would lend handle to the charge of India being an aggressor. But then Pakistan amassed its troops on India's western border and India had no option but to do likewise. Tension mounted. There were small skirmishes on both the eastern and western fronts.

But suddenly on the evening of Friday, 3 December 1971, the Pakistani air force delivered a pre-emptive strike on eight Indian airfields hoping to paralyse India's air force in one swoop. This was not only escalation but also miscalculation.

In the early hours of 4 December 1971, the prime minister of India went on the air to broadcast her message to the nation. 'I speak to you,' she said, 'at a moment of great peril to our country.

Some hours ago, soon after 5.30 pm on 3 December, Pakistan launched a full-scale war against us. The Pakistani air force suddenly struck at our airfields in Amritsar, Pathankot, Srinagar, Avantipur, Uttarlai, Jodhpur, Ambala and Agra. Their ground forces are shelling our defence positions in Sulaimanki, Khumkaran, Poonch and other sectors... Today, the war in Bangladesh has become a war on India; This has imposed upon me, my government and the people of India a great responsibility. We have no other option but to put our country on a war footing... Aggression must be met and the people of India will meet it with fortitude and determination and with discipline and utmost unity.'

The miscalculation led to severe retribution on several Pakistani airfields. Indian troops marched into Bangladesh, hand in hand with the *Mukti Vahini* and in the west made a deep thrust into Sind as well as Kashmir, though they suffered a temporary setback in the Chaamb sector. In the Arabian Sea, the Indian Navy won a signal victory over the Pakistani fleet in Karachi harbour, sinking three destroyers and damaging a fourth. One Pakistani submarine in the Bay of Bengal was also sunk.

In Bangladesh, hand in hand with the *Mukti Vahini*, the gallant Indian Army liberated one fortified town after another. Within a few days, Akhaura, Laksham, Feni, Sylhet, Jessore, Comilla and Dinajpur had fallen and the army converged from all sides towards Dacca. On 9 December, Pakistani Radio denied that Jessore and Comilla had fallen, but barely an hour later the BBC (British Broadcasting Corporation) announced that its correspondent who had gone to Jessore with the advancing Indian troops had reported that Jessore had fallen without even a fight and that the people had come out to welcome the Indian troops and the *Mukti Vahini*. Another BBC correspondent reported that as Indian troops closed in on Dacca, local civilians awaited their coming with hope.

Soon the skies of Bangladesh were cleared of all Pakistani air force planes and Chittagong harbour was pounded and isolated by the Indian Navy.

On 16 December 1971, the prime minister stated in Parliament: 'I have an announcement to make. The West Pakistani forces have unconditionally surrendered in Bangladesh.

The instrument of surrender was signed in Dacca at 16.31 hours IST today by Lt General A A K Niazi, on the behalf of the Pakistan Eastern Command. Lt General Jagjit Singh Arora, GOC-in-C of the Indian and Bangladesh forces in the Eastern Theatre accepted the surrender. Dacca is now the free capital... This house and the entire nation rejoice in this historic event. We hail the people of Bangladesh in their hour of triumph. We hail the brave young men and boys of the *Mukti Vahini* for their valour and dedication. We are proud of our own Army, Navy and Air Force and Border Security Force... Our objectives were limited—to assist the gallant people of Bangladesh and their *Mukti Vahini* to liberate their country from a reign of terror and to resist aggression on our own land. Indian Armed forces will not remain in Bangladesh any longer than is necessary... The triumph is not theirs alone. All nations who value the human spirit will recognise it as a significant milestone in man's quest for liberty.'

Next day, on 17 December 1971, Indira stated in Parliament that the previous evening she had instructed the Indian Army, Navy and Air Force to cease operations from 2000 hours on all fronts in the west. After the nine months of travail since the military crackdown of 25 March 1971, Bangladesh's struggle to be born was at an end.

Over also was the long night of anxiety about the fate of Sheikh Mujib-ur Rehman. After nine months, he was released from his solitary confinement in one of Pakistan's worst jails. Till the very last he neither asked pardon from his torturers nor flinched from his determination to secure his country's total independence. Z A Bhutto attempted to use his release as bait for a compromise that would keep Bangladesh in Pakistan. But all Mujib-ur Rehman said was he would have to ask his people to give a final answer. He was literally snatched from the jaws of death. President Yahya Khan had asked Bhutto to antedate his execution on the very morrow of the ceasefire. Very wisely, Bhutto refused to do so.

On his return to Dacca, where everyone was rejoicing, Sheikh Mujib-ur Rehman accepted the office of the prime minister of Bangladesh. He said in no uncertain terms that his country would have no links with Pakistan. Bangladesh was now a sovereign, independent republic and with Sheikh Mujib-ur Rehman, the father of the *Banglapita,* its prime minister.

EIGHTEEN

Magnanimous in Victory

War is a bloody and messy affair bringing death and destruction in its wake taking a fearful toll of lives from victors and vanquished alike. The Defence Ministry estimated that about 2,000 Indian soldiers were killed, 6,000 wounded and 1,600 missing; nine Indian pilots and three navigators lost their lives and nearly 200 civilians were killed as a result of Pakistani bombing and shelling. Pakistani casualties were higher and close to a lakh of their troops were in Indian custody.

In the border areas, especially in the Chaamb sector, the air was rent with the noise and din of battle as battalions advanced and retreated and tanks and airplanes were locked in fearful combat. Even Bombay, some distance away from the scene of battle, was not spared the fear and anxiety caused by the shrill warble of the sirens and the creeping darkness of the blackout that descended like a pall on the city. One fearful night, ack-ack guns went into action, barking like dogs, rocket flares lit up weirdly the night sky, sending down a hail of shells and shrapnel and Bombay had some idea of what war is like.

India was magnanimous in victory. After the crushing defeat of the Pakistani forces, India could well have imposed peace on its own terms. Such a peace would have been at the point of gun. Instead, the prime minister of India and the President of Pakistan met on the heights of Shimla in July 1972 decided to bury the hatchet. Atal Behari Vajpayee called this a 'sell-out'. But what other option was there for India but to forgo the spoils of victory and honour the self-respect of a neighboring country? How else could the Shimla Summit been salvaged but by India forgoing its pound of flesh in the interests of peace and good neighbourliness?

The two countries agreed to withdraw their forces from the occupied areas on the western border, except Jammu and Kashmir. This meant surrendering 5,200 square miles of Pakistani territory in return for 69 square miles occupied by Pakistan. True, the 5,200 miles were barren wastes of desert sand, and the 69 square miles of strategic importance. Still, in surrendering such large chunks of territory, India had made a generous gesture and President Bhutto could say before he left that the Shimla agreement had been a victory for both sides. The two sides also agreed to respect the ceasefire line. Diehards asked why India did not demand the return of Azad Kashmir, which had been occupied by Pakistan as a result of the invasion by Pushtu tribesmen after Partition of India in 1947. Pakistan still claimed that Kashmir belonged to it because of its Muslim majority. Bhutto agreed to freeze the situation and let Kashmir remain divided even though his people could not give up the right of Kashmiris to self-determination.

More important than the different clauses of the agreement was the spirit behind it. The two countries solemnly agreed to abjure the use of force, to renounce hate and seek the paths of peace and friendship. They were tired of the continuous barrage of hostile propaganda pouring from one country to the other. They wanted to understand each other better, to establish cultural exchanges, to let commerce flourish between them, allow people of one country to travel in the other and resume diplomatic relations with each other. The road ahead might be long but the journey would now be made as friends and brothers, not enemies. The two countries had too many vital internal problems to tackle and they could not afford to remain fixed in confrontation that had bedevilled relations between them during the last 25 years.

NINETEEN

The Restored Monolith

India's victory in the 14-day war with Pakistan was also Indira's personal triumph. Her support of the liberation forces that freed Bangladesh from an oppressive regime, her refusal to be hustled into a confrontation with Pakistan, the swiftness of the campaigns that forced Pakistan to surrender after its initial provocation—all these redounded upon her credit as not only India's but one of the world's greatest leaders. She stood head and shoulders above her rivals within her party and the country.

Already after the massive victory of the New Congress in the general elections all the Opposition parties had drifted into the doldrums. After the war, Indira as well as her party's supremacy was assured and unshakable.

In 1971, Indira Gandhi had received her mandate for undisputed leadership at the Centre, but now as the state assembly elections in March 1972 drew near, she wanted another mandate to show that her writ ran unchallenged in the 20 states that went to the polls.

The stakes might not have been as high as during the general elections. Yet, Indira took no chances. She went on a whirlwind tour of the whole country, devoting 29 days to her itinerary and delivering 185 speeches at 185 different places. The burden of her message was the same everywhere: *'Garibi Hatao'*, the need to eradicate poverty, but also, though she came basking in the glory of her victory over Pakistan, the need of eternal vigilance against external danger in the context of the Nixon-Chou communiqué.

The result was a foregone conclusion. Once again an Indira wave or rather an Indira typhoon swept over the land. All over the country people went to the polls stamping blindly on the cow and the calf, voting for Indira rather than their own local candidates. Local issues were largely forgotten in the enthusiasm to give the prime minister the mandate she wanted.

It was again a personal triumph for Indira. She had now in her grips the reins of power at the Centre as well as the states. In 12 of the 16 states, including West Bengal, where cadre of the Communist Party of India-Marxist (CPM) were creating trouble and in Jammu and Kashmir, she secured a majority of two-thirds and more; and a comfortable majority in Bihar, which had witnessed nine coalition governments in the previous elections.

The old Congress was reduced to a rump in its supposed strongholds of Gujarat and Mysore and wiped out completely in Maharashtra. The New Congress was now the only Congress and there was no other. The Swatantra Party too was wiped out and the Jana Sangh, the principal rival of the New Congress was ousted from Delhi and mauled in its stronghold in the Hindi heartland. The Socialists were decimated and the Communist Party of India (CPI) gained only where it had an electoral adjustment with the New Congress. Thus, the old monolithic Congress was restored.

But now there could be no excuses. If land reforms remained only on paper and the poor landless peasantry were not allowed to share the Green Revolution; if the drift to the towns was not arrested and slums continued to proliferate; if prices kept on rising and unemployment rate continued to grow; and if *Garibi Hatao* remained only a slogan, the blame would be laid fairly and squarely on the New Congress government. The economic survey showed the per capita income was no more than a rupee and the national income growth only four per cent. Industry was stagnant. There was no time to lose.

TWENTY

Twenty-Five Years of Independence

On 15 August 1972, the high domed Central Hall of Parliament reverberated with the speeches of remembrance and dedication; from the ramparts of the Red Fort was relived the memory of this first Independence Day 25 years before; hundreds of freedom fighters came to Delhi, received their *tamra patras*; parades and marches and flag salutations were held all over the country to celebrate the silver jubilee of India's Independence. There was splendour and beauty, grandeur and pageantry.

Brave and heroic speeches were made. The achievements of 25 years recounted. 'A quarter of a century has elapsed,' said Indira Gandhi at the midnight session of Parliament, 14–15 August, 'during which we have had our share of failure and success, of tragedy and triumphs. And yet we can take pride in the undeniable fact that despite the long sequences of challenges, we are today stronger—politically, economically and socially.

Our national unity, democracy, secularism and socialism remain strong and firm.'

But there was also a shadow over the celebrations, the shadow that falls between promise and fulfilment, the shadow of unemployment, rising prices and the fear of famine resulting from drought. Hence, the pledge of rededication to the ideals of the country. Our fight for Independence, said Indira, was not for ourselves alone but for all mankind. 'Let us rededicate ourselves not only to the service of India and her great people, but beyond to the broader goals of world peace and human welfare so that generations yet unborn can live with dignity and fulfilment as part of the great human family.' 'The greatness for which we strive,' she said, 'is not the greatness of military power or the avarice of economic exploitation. It is true greatness of the spirit. Only those who are free in spirit can be the torchbearers of freedom and the planners of the future.'

As though to emphasise the darkness of the shadow that falls between promise and fulfilment, in Bombay there was the indefinite civic strike that left mountains of garbage accumulating at street corners, roads littered with refuse and dirt, an all-pervading stink wherever one went, the water supply not very adequate at the best of times curtailed still further, government hospitals closed down, hundreds of sick people unattended and the BEST bus strike adding to the woes of commuters. Can one man or a few people, however powerful they may be, be allowed to hold a city to ransom with a strike timed to coincide with the silver jubilee celebration was the question. Whatever the demands of the workers, including a bonus for the BEST workers, justice had to be done to them but not at the cost of injustice to the six million people of Bombay.

However, even to this cloud, there was a silver lining. Just before the silver jubilee celebrations began came the news that prohibition was to be scrapped in Maharashtra. The law had been a costly mistake. Any good it may have achieved during the more than three decades the law had been in operation was more than counterbalanced by the awful degradation and wastage of human life that had resulted from it. Drunkenness was so rampant that a large proportion of those who drank became drunks. When unjust laws are forcibly imposed, then the lawmakers bring the law itself into disrepute and can hardly complain that it is being flouted. Such considerations perhaps were not exactly the reason why the law was now being scrapped. Mundane reasons like tourism or the drain on the state's finances for providing the apparatus to enforce prohibition probably had a greater influence in arriving at the decision.

TWENTY-ONE

The Battle for the
Colleges in Kerala

After the massive victory of the New Congress in the general as
well as the assembly elections, especially after India's victory in the
14-day war with Pakistan, it might have been thought that India
would now enter a period of greater stability and consolidation
and that development would have a greater priority over ideology.
However, even before the treaty with Pakistan was signed and very
much before the silver jubilee celebrations, ideology seems to have
become a major preoccupation, even to the extent of trying to water
down the Constitution.

On 9 February 1972, in Trivandrum (now Thiruvanan-
thapuram), the Union law minister, stated that the freedom granted
under the Constitution was being misused and he meant business
when he suggested amendment of minority rights in the Constitution to end malpractices in the field of education. The ruling
Congress party in Kerala also now thought it was time to push its
radicalism further in the direction of nationalisation by issuing an

Ordinance equalising student's fees in private colleges with those of state colleges. At the same time, it refused to increase the grant-in-aid to private colleges and ordered that if they were not opened by 3 July 1972, they would be disaffiliated from the university. This, in effect, meant that private colleges would find it impossible to continue.

Disaffiliating 120 colleges, while only 14 government colleges remained, meant practically the breakdown of the whole system of higher education in Kerala. Their take over by the government would run into conflict with the Article 30 (I) of the Constitution which guarantees to minorities the freedom to run 'educational institutions of their choice.' Sixty of these colleges were under Christian management.

The deadline for the opening of the colleges came and went and still 69 Christian and Nair colleges remained closed without the state government coming to any conclusion about how to take them over or what legislation to pass since it would conflict with the Constitution. Had the Kerala Pradesh Congress gone ahead with its plan of nationalisation, the whole state would be embroiled in a political crisis of the greatest magnitude.

Meanwhile, Cardinal Pareeattil, on behalf of the church and K Goplakrishna Pillai, on behalf of the Nair Service Society, sought the intervention of the prime minister to create an atmosphere in which the colleges under private agencies could function as before. The talks with the Kerala government and the private colleges however remained deadlocked over the appointment of teachers and the admission of students.

At a mammoth rally of Catholics in Ernakulam, Cardinal Pareeattil stated that the private agencies would not agree to any interference by the government, directly or indirectly, in their right of appointment of teachers. However, there would be no objection, he said, to the presence of 'observers' of the government and the University, who would 'observe' and give advice in the selection of teachers.

But the government was adamant. Home Minister K Karunakaran reiterated in Trivandrum on 18 July, the government's position: if it had to take responsibility for direct payment of staff in private colleges, it had to have control on the appointment of staff and admission of students. Indeed, Karunakaran went to Delhi to meet the prime minister and Chavan and other leaders at the Centre probably to sound them on some kind of ordinance to take over the private colleges. He was however advised, according to Express News Services, to try persuasion and negotiation instead of rushing through legislative measures or promulgating the ordinance.

The battle was now taken to the streets. Talks between the Liaison Committee and the managements had broken down. The sixty-nine private colleges still remained closed. In Ernakulam, Alleppey, Changanacherry, Quilon and Trichur, hundreds of thousands of teachers and students and others demonstrated against the government and the university. In Ernakulam, on Sunday 18 July, three lakh people defying the pouring rain marched from St Albert's College grounds to the sprawling Herbert grounds where they were addressed by Cardinal Pareeattil and other speakers.

Clearly the writing was on the wall. If the Congress did not change its stand, its days were numbered. Both the PSP and the Muslim League thought the stand of the Liaison Committee on the equalisation of fees in private and government colleges was inflexible and rigid. They were implicitly telling the Congress to climb down or else the government would topple. Moreover, the efforts of the government and the university to provide alternative colleges proved a farce. They were called 'Antony colleges' after the Congress leader Antony.

Finding they were fighting a losing battle, the Congress leaders air dashed to Hyderabad to meet the prime minister, who told them that she would help them to make alternative arrangements if no solution was possible. However, a new formula was suggested. It provided for a management-nominated five-member panel, with three representatives of the private colleges and two of the government for the recruitment of teachers. As for admissions, 30 per cent would be reserved for the Scheduled Castes and Scheduled Tribes, 10 per cent for the community owning the colleges, 20 per cent for the nominees of the management and the remaining on basis of merit. The Kerala government undertook to pay directly the salaries of teachers and the management to remit to the state treasuries, the standardised fees they had collected. The dispute was settled.

TWENTY-TWO

Ominous Portents

The settlement of the Kerala college dispute satisfied everyone, except the Marxists and the students' and youth wings of the Kerala Pradesh Congress Committee (KPCC) who had wanted to deprive the private management of control over their colleges and were talking of nationalising them and even amending the rights of minorities guaranteed by the Constitution. Obviously, the settlement was the direct result of the prime minister's personal intervention, her shrewd wisdom and practical judgement. But the question still remained why Union Law Minister H R Gokhale gave the initial push for the move to take over the private colleges and why he suggested amendment to the Constitution for this purpose. Was Gokhale part of that extreme Left wing of the Congress, which was for more and more nationalisation and more and more changes in the Constitution? Was the country drifting towards Communism?

The question might have seemed alarmist, but there were portents that indicated such a drift.

The Calcutta session of the Congress seemed to indicate that both the country and the party were back to square one. Once again there was evidence of factionalism within the party, the Young Turks throwing the blame for the lack of progress on the moderates. Once again the same old ideological battle cries were heard even though the country was in no mood to listen to slogan shouters. And, once again there was the same disarray within the party's rank and file, bogus membership having found a chance apparently without difficulty. The hunt for power was still the game the New Congress was playing, without knowing apparently how that power was to be used.

And, to cover up its omissions and commissions, there was the search for alibis. Powerful nations, it was said, were out to prevent the progress of the country, the CIA was engaged in sabotage and the Grand Alliance of opposition parties was mustering its forces and exploiting the situation for its own purposes.

Another ominous portent was the massive rally of half-a-million people at the Boat Club in New Delhi organised by the CPI. Most of them had come ticketless from hundreds of miles away. Who waived the green flag for them? The prime minister? The union minister? The purpose of the rally was to bring down prices, enforce the ceilings on land, end unemployment, take over the wholesale grain trade and nationalise what had not been nationalised. The rally was a threat that unless these reforms were carried out, there would be violent revolution.

What did the prime minister and the Congress leaders think of all the gratuitous aid offered to their own policies. Surprisingly, the prime minister, it was said, had herself been appealing to various Left elements to join hands with the Congress to further the cause of socialism. Her new Home Minister Uma Shankar Dikshit, in his first major speech in Parliament, said: 'There is common ground between the Communist Party and ourselves because they stand for socialism. Ultimately, the aim of Communism is socialism. Let anybody deny it...' And, Union Health Minister R K Khadilkar said that collaboration between the Communists and the Congress should be strengthened for the common good of the country. The CPI on its part was ready and willing for the alliance. In its fight to defeat the Rightist counter-offensive and bring about a shift to the Left, said the CPI National Council report, its main allies would be the progressive sections inside the Congress and the masses following the Congress.

The conclusion that emerged was clear. The Congress seemed to be heading for a split. Right reaction would be purged and only the radical Left, left. Between these and the CPI there was no difference and a marriage could be easily settled. But the CPI being what it was, would it remain content being just a partner and not the sole survivor?

Perhaps the most serious portent of a drift towards totalitarian despotism was the Supreme Court judgement in April 1973 giving Parliament the right to amend any article of the Constitution including the Fundamental Rights. Our Constitution was the ultimate court of appeal for the safeguarding of our democracy and all three—the legislature, the executive and the judiciary—were to work within the framework of the Constitution and it was the section of Fundamental Rights that was declared to be the most sacred and inviolable.

The Part III of the Indian Constitution that contains Fundamental Rights was declared inviolable by the Constitution itself so that the Fundamental Human Rights that are sacred in a democracy may be guaranteed to every citizen. The Article 13(2) of the Indian Constitution says very clearly that the State (and that includes Parliament) 'shall not make any law which takes away or abridges the rights conferred by this Part (Part III) and any law made in contravention of this clause shall to the extent of this contravention be void.'

By giving Parliament the power to amend any part of the Constitution, the Supreme Court made Parliament omnipotent and reduced the Constitution to a scrap of paper. Should a Communist government or any other government with a steamroller majority in Parliament come to power and have the right to amend or abrogate any or all of the articles of the Constitution, it could abolish even the Fundamental Human Rights and use the Constitution to subvert the Constitution.

Already in June 1971, soon after the general elections H R Gokhale informed the Rajya Sabha that the Union Cabinet was giving urgent and 'serious consideration' to amend the Constitution and to implement programmes for economic and social justice.

Some appraisals of the government's intentions suggested that the Right to Property in the Constitution was to be diluted or qualified and that the Supreme Court's jurisdiction to intervene on the issue of fair compensation and breach of the Fundamental Right to property was to be excluded. 'This,' said an editorial in *The Hindustan Times*, 'would be going far beyond the mandate received by Indira Gandhi... Any move to bring on the Statute Book Expropriatory Legislation that is not subject to the scrutiny of the courts could spell danger to Parliamentary democracy as understood in this country.' Other reports suggested that government intended to follow its bill for the amendment of Article 368 that deals with amendment process, with another bill to delete the Article 13(2) of the Constitution. Parliamentarian J M Soho Prabhu argued that the Article 13(2) could not coexist with the amendment proposed to the Article 368 and as long as the Article 13(2) existed Fundamental Rights could not be touched.

By granting Parliament the right to amend any article of the Constitution, including Part III, the Supreme Court had set aside the Article 13(2). Chief Justice A K Sikri and six of the judges were convinced that there were limitations to Parliament's amending powers. Parliament does not have the power to abrogate Fundamental Rights, but it can amend, adjust or regulate them as long as the rights are not destroyed in the process. Similarly, the amount given as compensation for acquired property for a public purpose should not be illusory.

However, five of the judges held that the powers of Parliament to amend Constitution are unlimited and Fundamental Rights can, therefore, be abrogated.

Swift on the heels of the Supreme Court judgement on Parliament's power to amend any article of the Constitution came the appointment of a Chief Justice of the Supreme Court, A N Ray this move was declared politically motivated by Justice A K Sikri. In the process the claims of three other judges, Justice Hegde, Justice Grover and Justice Shellat, were set aside ignoring a well-established convention that the office should go to the senior most of the Supreme Court judges.

Why then was Justice A N Ray preferred to others? The reason was these three, while conceding Parliament's right to amend any article of the Constitution, went on to declare that this did not include a right to abrogate any of the Fundamental Rights or to go against the basic framework of the Constitution. Also, they said the compensation paid for acquired property should have some proportion to the property acquired and they struck down the amendment that would delegate to the state legislature the power to amend Fundamental Rights. Justice Ray, on the other hand, would not impose the slightest limitation on Parliament's amending powers and he found nothing wrong with the amendment that was struck down.

Any wonder then that the executive found in Justice Ray's position just what it wanted from a Chief Justice of the Supreme Court? Any wonder also that his appointment was made with a view to securing 'a committed judiciary' as had been desired several times during the previous two years by the executive?

In the Lok Sabha, Frank Anthony charged that the appointment had been made because of biased Steel Minister Mohan Kumaramangalam and Law Minister H R Gokhale against the senior judges. At a press conference, one of the superseded judges, Justice Shellat, described the appointment as a 'blow to democracy' and said that it had destroyed the 'entire' fabric of judiciary and its 'indispensable independence.'

TWENTY-THREE

Indira's Worries

When India celebrated the 25th anniversary of its Independence on 15 August 1972, Indira Gandhi was at the height of her power and greatness. She had won sweeping victories in the general as well as state elections. The making of Bangladesh and the victory over Pakistan in the 14 day war were rightly seen as redounding to her credit. Her speech at the midnight session of Parliament was the highlight of the silver jubilee celebrations. Why then barely six months later in 1973, did she rush into amendments of the Constitution and other measures that seemed to suggest that she wanted still more power in her hands?

Obviously she was worried. She said her enemies were forming a 'grander alliance' and carrying on a smear campaign against her. But did she not have a steamroller majority in Parliament as well as in the states. Why did she have to bother about what anybody might say or do? True, but then she had promised to banish poverty and her plans for doing so did not seem to have even got off the ground. Prices were shooting up and the people were getting restive. The tide seemed to have begun to turn, the Indira wave to recede. So she looked for alibis.

One of her big worries in March 1973 was the poor showing of her Congress Party in the elections to the Bombay Municipal Corporation. After the general and the state elections she and her top men had taken a runaway victory in the civic elections for granted. They were in for a rude shock. Out of 140 seats the Congress had secured only 45.

What had gone wrong? Indira sent for Rajani Patel, the leader of the Party organisation in Bombay. Patel rushed to Delhi and probably blamed the whole collapse on the sectarian religious passions roused by the attempt to make the Muslims sing the pre-Independence song, *Vande Mataram* (I worship the Mother), in their schools. The Muslims had taken strong objection to the move, saying they would worship no one but Allah and voted *en masse* for their communal party, Muslim League.

The Hindus on the other hand voted for their own communal parties, the Jana Sangh and the Shiv Sena. Sectarian passions were no doubt part of the reason for the Congress debacle. So greatly had passions been inflamed that victory processions of the rival parties clashed, there was large-scale rioting and looting, two Muslims were killed. But a more profound reason was to be found in the Congress itself. Ever since the 1971 elections, the organisational wing of the Bombay Congress had been at loggerheads with the legislative wing. The older Congress leaders had not taken kindly to the imposition by Indira on the party organisation of well-known Communist leaders like Rajani Patel, who overnight became Congressmen. Many of them then worked actively for Opposition candidates and sabotaged the elections.

Indeed, at the Centre as well as the states, the old story of infighting in the Congress ranks was repeating itself. Some of the new men whom Indira put in power had, Communist or fellow travelling backgrounds. Communists, it was being openly said, found it easier to rise to power by becoming Congressmen than by staying in their own party. The older Congress members naturally resented this, when they could not stand it any longer, rebelled.

In Orissa, large section of Congressmen defected from the party, bringing down the government and necessitating the imposition of the President's Rule on the state. They just could not work any longer under Chief Minister Nandini Satpathy, whom Indira Gandhi had foisted on them. In Andhra Pradesh, several Congressmen rebelled against P V Narasimha Rao, yet another nominee of Indira Gandhi, and worked for the bifurcation of the state against the prime minister's known wishes. Similarly, a signature campaign was afoot in Gujarat against the Chief Minister, Ghanashyam Oza. Seventy of the 139 strong Congress Legislature Party held a meeting under Planning Minister Chimanbhai Patel to demonstrate their strength. Oza who was Indira's nominee, lost majority and had to demit the office. Once again, Oza was a nominee of the prime minister. Gujarat was a Congress stronghold but factionalism had done its work and the fortress was now in ruins. In Bihar and Uttar Pradesh, it was the same story. Some central ministers were encouraging factionalism.

In Bihar, Indira nominated Kedar, but was ousted by a faction that had the support of a central minister. In Uttar Pradesh, Kamlapati Tripathi was insisting he would not resign because of the Provincial Arms Constabulary (PAC) revolt, for which he was being blamed, ultimately he bowed out under the pressure. Instead of appointing another Congress leader, the Centre stepped in and brought Uttar Pradesh under the President's Rule. States like Bihar and Uttar Pradesh remained under-developed, but power-hungry politicians thought of nothing but their own selfish interests. Inefficiency and corruption were rampant and the country seemed to be in great turmoil.

The most important reason for the rout of the Congress in the Bombay civic elections was that many people were fed up with it. Significantly, the '*Garibi Hatao*' slogan did not feature in the Congress electioneering propaganda. How could it? In a few months, prices of food and essential commodities had risen by 25 per cent. Agricultural and industrial production had slowed down due to acute power shortage. The Green Revolution that promised prosperity through enhanced productivity had not materialised. Total production of food grains slumped from 104.68 million tons in 1971–72 to about 96 million tons in 1972–73.

To be fair to the late prime minister, it must be pointed out that one year or even two years were not enough to banish poverty from the land. Moreover, she seemed to have struck a patch of bad luck. The monsoons failed, causing acute drought conditions in most states of the central India. In Maharashtra, 24 out of 26 districts were in the grip of scarcity and eight under real famine. Some 20 million people, it was estimated had been affected. A few starvation deaths may have been reported, but there could be no doubt that millions were suffering from malnutrition. Rivers dried up. Wells were empty and not a patch of grass was to be seen for miles. Cattle were sold for as little as Rs 25 per head and trains crowded to the full with drought-stricken people flocked to Bombay and other cities, adding to the overcrowding in the slums.

Government started relief works and four million people were expected to be benefitted by them by the time the rains came again. Their main purpose was to provide water in the short term and lay the infrastructure for agricultural development in the long term. By the end of February 1973, about 300 community wells had been dug up and work was in progress on another 3,000. The idea was to have deep tube wells (about 250 to 300 feet), which alone could provide water, throughout the drought-stricken districts. The target was to have a tube well within five miles of every village.

Unfortunately, there was a shortage of deep drilling rigs. Apart from the wells, some 500 irrigation and percolation tanks were completed with work in progress on another 1,000, one million hectares were contour-bunded and the earthwork was finished for a road length of nearly 50 thousand kilometre.

Workers were paid Rs 2.50 a day to buy their meagre rations. Over one million workers were being given a supplementary protein-rich meal of wheat flour, jaggery and mineral and vitamin additives. Voluntary agencies like the Caritas India and the US Catholic Relief Services joined the government in the fight against famine. Many missionaries worked with the drought-stricken on the relief works.

But drought or no drought, Indira's critics said that it was to meet problems related to monsoons that the Five-Year Plans were devised. In spite of four such plans, the country seemed to be no nearer to a solution. Instead of the nationalisation of coal mines or of taking over the wholesale trade in food grains, Indira would have done far better had she taken a hard decision and achieved a substantial increase in food grain production. But of that there seemed to be no hopeful signs.

To add to the woes, there was the population problem. With two per cent of the world's land, India had 14 per cent of the world's people. In 1973, the population of India was 550 millions. By 2000, it was estimated to be a billion. All the efforts of the country to increase food supply and other amenities to better the quality of life of our people were being negated by the growth in the numbers. We have to keep running, Indira said, only to stand still.

Population growth was only one of the many factors arresting human development in India. Inadequate food supply, bad housing, poor education, unemployment, social inequalities and a host of other factors tended to depress the socio-economic environment, which in turn reacted on the growth of population. The only solution was an integrated plan of socio-economic development that could include family planning as an important element.

At the International Conference on Population Growth and Human Development held at the Indian Social Institute in Delhi in late November 1973, Vice President of India, G S Pathak, pointed out that the problem was basically a human problem. Any move to bring about a reduction in numbers by ignoble methods, such as forced sterilisation, were not in keeping with human dignity and must be rejected. The policy of the government, said Pathak, was that family planning should be voluntary.

In his address at the valedictory function, Jayaprakash Narayan pointed out that official family planning had been a failure because the field workers were wrongly motivated. Targets had been earmarked for the village doctor or the block development officer for so many vasectomies, tubectomies or other birth-control devices. Such methods only defeated their own ends. They led to falsification of registers and worse still, the coercion of poor villagers by officials.

The problem, in Jayaprakash Narayan's opinion, would not be solved until a safe, cheap and simple method of birth control had been developed. Already there was a change of heart among the people for the small family norm. Whereas formerly more children were thought to be needed for helping in the family business, today, he said, parents were realising that if they gave their children a good education, there was a chance of raising their own standards of living. But such education would not be possible if there were too many children. But an effective method of family planning was still not available to them.

A lighter moment at the conference had come when one of the lady participants herself not very young had gone to the rostrum and recited the nursery rhyme:

'There was an old woman

Who lived in a shoe

She had so many children

She didn't know what to do

She gave them some broth

Without any bread

And whipped them all soundly

And sent them to bed.'

Fr. Arthur McCormack, M H M a demographic expert, soon after said he only wanted to add one word to the rhyme:

'She had so many children

Because she did not know what to do.'

Clearly, population was not the least of Indira's worries.

TWENTY-FOUR

The JP Movement

Time was running out for the country and its government. The 1974 economic survey painted a dismal picture of the economy. The wholesale price index rose by 26 per cent in 1973 following a 14 per cent rise in 1972. Industrial production was stagnant, power generation had declined, food reserves were down and food procurement disappointing.

The overall rate of growth during the Fourth Five-Year Plan was less than 3.5 per cent as compared to the target of 5.7 per cent. Unemployment figures kept on mounting and the terms of trade moved ominously against the country. The budget showed a deficit of Rs 125 crore. The spectre of inflation had raised its ugly head.

Time was running out for the country. What the food riots in Gujarat demonstrated was that the patience of people was wearing thin. In a year of bumper harvests, the people of India could have hoped for some respite, but bread had been snatched from their mouths due to inefficiency, hoarding and corruption of countless men both within the government and outside.

Soaring prices and inflationary pressures were being felt everywhere due to the oil and energy crisis. But in India the crisis was one of morality and the other of human greed.

In Gujarat, for over three months, processions, demonstrations, mock funerals, *gheraos, dharnas* and fasts had become the order of the day. The agitation against the corrupt and faction-ridden Chimanbhai Patel Government took a toll of over a hundred lives, besides massive destruction of property. Ultimately, the Nav Nirman Samiti of Gujarat students brought the Patel government down and the President's Rule was imposed. In February 1974, Jayaprakash Narayan, on whom the mantle of Mahatma Gandhi had fallen, visited Gujarat to meet the Nav Nirman Samiti students, teachers and the workers of Gujarat Sarvodaya Mandal to study the situation.

Addressing a '*Lok Swaraj Sammelan*' conference convened by the Gujarat Sarvodaya Mandal, Jayaprakash advised students, teachers and the Sarvodaya workers to approach people and convince them to put moral pressure on the elected legislators (MLAs) to resign. The assembly would then be dissolved, he said. He urged them, however, not to force resignation by *gheraos* or shouting slogans at their residences. He appealed to college students to give up their classes for a year and work for a 'youth revolution.'

Jayaprakash came, saw and conquered. He praised and chided the students alternatively, and they listened to him in pin-drop silence. But he had to leave for his own state of Bihar and though the Gujarat State Assembly was later dissolved as he had forecast, the students went back to college and there was nothing left in Gujarat but the President's Rule.

In Ahmedabad, Jayaprakash saw a ray of hope in student and people's power. Much as he might have disapproved of the methods used, he admired the courage of the youth and students of Gujarat. Soon the students of Patna and Bihar also came to Jayaprakash to ask for his guidance and leadership.

In Bihar too, for over five weeks, processions, *gheraos*, demonstrations and *dharnas* were the order of the day. Bihar erupted into an orgy of looting and violence which was followed by police firing. Twenty people were killed in Patna and 10 in Gaya.

The trouble began on 18 March 1974. Around 10 thousand students poured into Patna. Their *gherao* of the Bihar Legislative Assembly led to a clash with the police. In 10 days of chaos, more was destroyed in Bihar than in two months of the Gujarat agitation. Government offices, hotels, restaurants, petrol pumps, shops, railway stations, houses of officials and ministers, and the offices of two newspapers *Searchlight* and *Pradeep* were set ablaze. Curfew had to be clamped on eight cities.

No one should have been surprised by this turn of events in Bihar. Forty per cent of its people lived below the poverty line. The gap between the few rich landlords and the vast majority of tenant farmers was enormous. Riddled with caste, Bihar's politics had been notoriously unstable, one government toppling after another as the game of floor crossing went merrily on. Chief Minister Abdul Ghafoor could not weld the heterogeneous ministry set up 10 months earlier to give representation to various conflicting interests and the result was inefficiency and mismanagement. Worst of all, corruption was rampant and many Cabinet ministers were the worst offenders. Now with prices soaring, essential commodities in short supply and unemployment mounting, the patience of the people exhausted as it did in Gujarat. Students spearheaded the agitation to overthrow the Ghafoor ministry and dissolute the Legislative Assembly. Their demands for better education and for curbing corruption along with unemployment and checking the soaring prices had been met with an unresponsive attitude by the Bihar government.

It was because Jayaprakash Narayan saw very clearly that a mere reshuffling of the Cabinet was not enough that he had launched his non-political, non-violent crusade for a 'moral revolution.' 'Unless corruption is brought under control,' he said, 'even the best socio-economic policies will go wrong and no-ism, socialism or any other, can have any chance. In fact, the nation itself may decay and die or be enslaved again.'

That the agitation was non-violent except on two occasions was due largely to Jayaprakash Narayan. Even the shooting in Gaya was perpetrated on a wholly non-violent crowd. The most eloquent witness of the non-violence of Jayaprakash's (JP's) movement was the unique procession of silent peace marchers through the streets of Patna on 8 April. Their lips sealed with saffron cloth and their hands clasped behind their backs, the processionists marched behind placards saying: 'Our hearts are filled with sorrow, but our tongues are tied. The ruling party is responsible for the galloping prices, rampant corruption, mounting unemployment and prevailing scarcity. Whatever the form of attack on us, we will not lift one little finger in retaliation.' After such a promise Jayaprakash Narayan could go to Vellore for his operation without fear of any violence erupting.

But close on the heels of the Gujarat and Bihar turmoil came the railway men's strike. All over the country trains came to a halt. In Bombay, thousands had to go to work taking whatever means of transport they could get, waiting for long hours in the sweltering May heat at bus stops, packing buses, trucks and tempos like sardines and arriving two or three hours late in a half-empty office or factory, marking attendance and then going through the same process on the way back home. The *Bharat Bandh* (All India Strike) on 15 May 1974, came almost as a relief from this mindless ordeal.

Meanwhile, All India Radio and the newspapers kept on announcing that more trains were running, railway workers were returning to duty, new hands were being employed and rail traffic was being cleared in the great railway junctions like Mughalserai. The strike it was said would fizzle out. On the other hand, it was reported that 15,000 railway men had been arrested, that striking workers were threatened they would lose their jobs and their quarters, that drivers and motormen were being forced to report on duty and that George Fernandes had gone on a hunger strike in jail to protest against the repression of railway men. In Parliament, the prime minister and the railway minister defended the government's position and the Opposition walked out unceremoniously.

Doubtless, the railway men had legitimate grievances. Their pay scales were low and they got no bonuses, when even private companies running at a loss did. But they got free railway passes, decent accommodation, special grain shops and free medical care in railway hospitals. Granting them bonuses would spur other government undertakings to make similar demands and cost, according to the union leaders Rs 300 crore but Rs 500 crore according to the government. This was enough to throw the whole economy into chaos.

The situation called for patient negotiations but neither the government nor the union leaders were in a mood to compromise. Even while the talks were being held, a strike notice was given and even before they broke off, George Fernandes and other union leaders were arrested. Opposition parties, including the Jana Sangh and the Marxists exploited the strike for their own purposes, hoping that it would lead to a revolt of the masses that would overthrow the regime. George Fernandes was reported to have been talking about a revolution, violent if necessary, that would dissolve Parliament and frame a new Constitution for the country.

There was no violent revolution but time was running out for Indira Gandhi and her government. JP's movement was gathering momentum and, if unchecked, would spread from Bihar to Uttar Pradesh, Haryana and the Punjab. In Parliament, no business was being done due to obstructionist Opposition tactics. The economic situation continued to deteriorate. The scheduled date for the next general elections was mere a year away in 1976. To wait till then would make it difficult for Indira to win with as large a majority as in 1971. Meanwhile, the Opposition was still in disarray. So, it was said, Indira had decided to strike while the iron was hot and go in for a snap poll while the going was good. To put life into the Congress party, new Congress president Dev Kant Barooah went round organising training camps.

The Opposition, too, geared up for a possible snap poll. The old Congress and the Socialists held national assemblies to hammer out a strategy to fight the elections. Even Jayaprakash Narayan said Indira's election challenge would be taken up. He, however, asked the leaders of his movement only to organise the Opposition to the Congress but not to stand for elections.

People were not in a mood for elections. What good would an election do to the millions of the suffering and poverty stricken who had been oppressed and exploited by corrupt, venal and power-seeking politicians? Big money, communal and caste loyalties might perhaps buy their votes as they had done in the assembly elections in Uttar Pradesh and Orissa where the Congress had won by a slender majority a year ago. But how representative were those elected of the wishes of the people? It was precisely to avoid the influence of too much money power that the Representation of People's Act 1951 had laid it down that election expenses of parliamentary candidates should not exceed Rs 25,000. The ruling had been interpreted as referring only to personal not party expenses. The Supreme Court attempted to set the matter right by declaring that it included party expenses also when it set aside the election of A N Chawla, Congress MP from Delhi whereupon the government quickly passed a Presidential Ordinance amending the Representation of People's Act, Section 77 to nullify the Supreme Court judgment. The country was back to square one.

There was no snap poll but JP's movement was gathering a greater momentum. As the general elections drew near, the Congress party decided to meet JP's challenge head on. The President's address to the Parliament was strongly critical of JP's movement in Bihar. The late prime minister herself termed the Oppositions 'fascist' and accused it of indulging in Hitlerite methods. She blamed JP's movement for creating an atmosphere of violence.

On the other hand, JP's movement was spreading to other states like Uttar Pradesh, Madhya Pradesh and Haryana. On 19 February 1975, JP gave the call for a 'people's march' to the Parliament on 6 March. Speaking to students in Patna, he charged Indira with contemplating the setting up of a Bangladesh-type of dictatorship in the country. Preparations were on, he said, for the demonstration before Parliament on 6 March. 'The movement,' he said, 'is to begin on a big scale in Uttar Pradesh after 6 March. The movement is to be revived in Gujarat. There will be countrywide observance of revoke Emergency day in state capitals and other towns chosen for this purpose.'

Indira Gandhi and Jayaprakash Narayan seemed to be set on a collision course. Things were heading for a showdown. Just then the three Young Turks from the Congress; Chandrasekhar, Krishna Kant and Mohan Daria, appealed for a dialogue. It was feared the Congress Party would discipline these three for having had the courage of their convictions and speaking out boldly about what they thought was the path of sanity. The CPI and those Communists who were now in the Congress clearly intended to split the Congress Party and isolate the anti-Communist forces so as to share power with like-minded cronies in the Congress Party. They attacked Jagjivan Ram, T A Pai and Subramaniam and called for an all out war on JP's movement, which they described as reactionary and counter-revolutionary.

Indira Gandhi, on her part, was not identified with any one section of the Congress. Ideologically, she often differed from the extreme left as her defence of T A Pai's statement about public participation in the public sector showed. But she indicted JP's movement in Bihar as being unconstitutional and therefore undemocratic, and refused to yield on the question of dissolving the Bihar Assembly. She also questioned why students were told to keep away from their studies for so long, where exactly the Bihar movement was heading and whether it would not create more confusion and anarchy than before. She charged that Opposition parties like the Jana Sangh had climbed on JP's bandwagon and were exploiting the movement to win power for themselves and embarrass the government.

On the other hand, there could be no underestimating the strength of JP's movement and the power behind the protest against corruption. True the inflationary spiral had slowed down somewhat due to the credit squeeze, the crackdown on hoarding and the fairly good harvest. But the Balance of Payments (BoP) gap was as wide as ever due to the fuel crisis. Not all the ills of the country could be blamed on the government, but so long as corruption was rampant and the voting system encouraged such corruption, the government would be blamed for failing to deliver and for not redeeming its promise of banishing poverty and land reforms it had made during the 1971 elections.

If the Bihar movement had gathered such momentum, it was because the Bihar government had forfeited its right to rule. Indira Gandhi's own popularity had waxed. She realised that it was because of JP's movement. That is why she took such an intransigent stand towards him.

However, not all the doors for dialogue for which the Young Turks had called were closed. Indira Gandhi herself told a Congress Parliamentary Party meeting that she did not relish Congress members branding Jayaprakash Narayan as a fascist. She was prepared for a meaningful dialogue with the Opposition on electoral law reform and other issues in the national interest. Her vision of a change in the 'quality of life' of the people was not so far away from Jayaprakash's concept of 'total revolution'. Also, in his address to both houses of Parliament, President V V Giri assured the members that the government was anxious to enact the Lok Pal and the Lok Ayukta Bill and would discuss with the leaders of political parties proposals for changes in the electoral law and 'far-reaching' educational reforms.

TWENTY-FIVE

The Allahabad High Court Bombshell

Efforts to bring the two sides together came to an end when an exasperated Morarji Desai went on an indefinite fast to protest the continuous postponement of state elections in Gujarat and the Centre yielded and agreed to hold them before the rains started. Gujarat had been under President's Rule for over a year after the students' Nav Nirman Samiti had brought Chimanbhai Patel's New Congress government down.

The agitation against the corrupt and faction-ridden government had lasted for nearly three months, taking a toll of over a hundred lives and large-scale destruction of property. But elections were being postponed time and again, and on one pretext or another, the last being the drought conditions in the state. The battle lines were now clearly drawn and all the top leaders in the country campaigned for one side or the other. The Opposition parties united in the Janata Front and Jayaprakash Narayan, Morarji

Desai, Atal Behari Vajpayee and local leaders, like Babubhai Patel, threw their weight into the battle. On the Congress side, Indira Gandhi covered hundreds of miles in her helicopter and addressed large crowds, mostly of women, promising them stability.

The eyes of the country were fixed on Gujarat but even before the election results could be declared, the Allahabad High Court judgement burst like a bombshell, throwing the Gujarat elections into the shade.

The lessons of the elections were clear. The Congress had its strength reduced by half and came out as an also-ran. The bitter infighting and the stigma of corruption, which remained even after Chimanbhai Patel was thrown out of the Congress, had taken its toll. Had it not been for Indira Gandhi's appeal to the tribals and the rural population, the Congress would not have won 41 per cent of the votes cast, though it lost its majority of seats in the assembly.

The other lesson was that the unity of the various parties in the Janata Front had paid off. They pooled their resources in support of the common candidates and won 86 of the 162 assembly seats and with the help of the Kisan Mazdoor Lok Paksha (KMLP) could form a government under Babubhai Patel. The third lesson was that what the people wanted was a clean and efficient administration, unlike those that had so long been in power and sought only the loaves and fishes of power.

As was said earlier, the Gujarat election results were completely overshadowed by the Allahabad High Court judgement in the middle of June 1975. The court set aside Indira Gandhi's election to Parliament in 1971 as void. She had used gazetted government officers to set up rostrums and supply power for their campaign in Rai Bareili and engaged the services of Yashpal Kapoor as her secretary when he was still a gazetted central government officer. Indira was found guilty of 'corrupt election practices' and could no longer continue as prime minister, though a stay order of 20 days was granted.

Immediately there ensued a heated debate whether Indira should stay or go. She herself said that local governments had made arrangements for election meetings even in her father's time. In any case, it was an opposition Samyukta Vidhayak Dal (SVD) government, then in power, that had made the arrangements in Rai Bareili. Her secretary Yashpal Kapoor had ceased drawing his salary from 14 January 1971.

Congress Party leaders, especially Barooah, left no stone unturned to convince everybody that Indira Gandhi should stay. She had not been convicted, they argued, of 'moral turpitude' but only on minor technical grounds. If Indira Gandhi were asked to quit on points of such petty details, few members of Parliament would be able to retain their seats. Moreover, Indira Gandhi could ask the Supreme Court for another stay order after the first had elapsed.

Congress leaders argued that the country could ill afford to lose Indira's guiding hand at the juncture. There were dangers from within and without. The economy was in precarious condition; neither in the government nor in the Opposition was there a leader of comparable stature. That she was still the undisputed leader of the masses, who wanted her to stay, was evident from the enormous crowds that flocked to her residence from distant villages of Punjab and Haryana to express their fullest confidence in her. Messages were pouring in from all parts of the country, entreating her to stay.

On 18 June, 451 out of over 500 members of the Congress Parliamentary Party amidst thunderous applause passed a unanimous resolution expressing their 'fullest faith and confidence in Indira' and their firm belief that 'her continued leadership as prime minister is indispensable to the nation.' Indira said that the resolution proposed by Jagjivan Ram and seconded by Y V Chavan, symbolised the resurgent India of today and the aspirations of her people. 'Now more than ever the Congress and the nation need her leadership and guidance.'

The Opposition on the other hand argued that the verdict of the Allahabad High Court was clear and unambiguous. There were no such things as minor or technical offences. Indira had contravened the election rules and had, therefore, been unseated. No candidate could have an unfair advantage over others, not even the prime minister. The law was law and must take its course. No individual was above the law. To disregard the law in the name of the people was undemocratic.

The stay order had been given for Indira to appoint a successor as her counsel had asked. For her, to use it to dig in her heels was proof that she had got the stems under false pretences.

She could not now ask for a second stay order. Even if that were granted there would now, after the amendment of fundamental rights and the supercession of Supreme Court judges, be the suspicion that it was granted by a committed judiciary. That is why, Opposition leaders said, they had staged a *dharna* near the Rashtrapati Bhavan (President's Office) to declare openly that they did not acknowledge Indira as the prime minister any longer.

As regards the crowds that flocked to the prime minister's residence, the Opposition leader asked how spontaneous they were, brought by the truckload from distant villages and left stranded in Delhi with no transport for their return. That Indira Gandhi had lost the confidence of the masses was shown by the Congress defeat in the Gujarat elections. With JP's movement still retaining its momentum, the Gujarat elections might have proved to be a rehearsal for the general elections.

So, the debate went on.

TWENTY-SIX

The Emergency

The debate over Indira's disqualification was soon brought to a close in a dramatic fashion. On 26 June 1975, she went on the air and announced to a stunned nation: 'The President has proclaimed Emergency. This is nothing to panic about. I am sure you are all conscious of the deep and widespread conspiracy, which has been brewing ever since I began certain progressive measures and benefits to the common man and woman of India.'

The panic was clear in her mind. All that talk about sinister forces conspiring to throw her out and the country going to pieces, were she to step down, was only a cloak to cover up her unabashed clinging to power in the face of the Allahabad High Court judgement. Rushing through the amendment to the Representation of People's Act in an Opposition-less Parliament and giving it retroactive effect had rendered her own appeal to the Supreme Court for another stay order redundant. Parliament, instead of the Supreme Court, had given the verdict: Mrs Gandhi had always been the prime minister and always would be. On 8 August 1975, Parliament confirmed Indira Gandhi as prime minister of India, notwithstanding the Allahabad High Court judgement.

With the Supreme Court appeal now out of the way, the Emergency could be theoretically prolonged till doomsday. Nor, so long as it lasted, did elections have to be held though they were due the following February in 1976. But time and again Indira Gandhi repeated that the Emergency would only last so long as it was necessary and there had been too strong a democratic tradition within her family for her to come out openly as a dictator. She still had a hold on the masses and if she could show that she had brought prices down, made rice and food grains and other essentials available especially to the vulnerable sections of the people, then she would be able to persuade the masses that she had fulfilled her promises of '*Garibi Hatao*' (banish poverty) to the best of her ability. She would be able to ride to power again on the crest of another Indira wave and be once more a democratically elected prime minister.

Meanwhile, as long as the Emergency lasted democracy was dead or at least in a state of suspended animation. By mid-August, in less than two months, 10 thousand people had probably been arrested all over the country under the Maintenance of Internal Security Act (MISA) without any reason being ascribed and left to languish in prison without trial. Doubtless, many of these were notorious smugglers, hoarders, black marketeers or members of extremist groups like the Naxalites, the Rashtriya Swayamsewak Sangh (RSS) and the Anand Margis, which were banned. Many of them were political prisoners, such as Morarji Desai, Jayaprakash Narayan, Ashoka Mehta and Piloo Modi. They were arrested in one fell midnight swoop for no other reason than that they happened to be leaders of the Opposition. Some of these men had spent longer years in prison before Independence and done as much if not more than Indira for their country and could lay greater claim to a share in the mantle of the Mahatma than her. Other Opposition leaders, such as George Fernandes, went underground and dared not come out into the open lest they should be clapped in jail. Even members of the Congress Party were told to toe the line or get out.

All public meetings were banned and anyone overheard in train or restaurant uttering even a hint of criticism was likely to be whisked off into police custody. Crushing boredom invaded the newspapers, which carried identical censored news items and commented longwindedly about affairs in every other country but their own. Foreign magazines, like *Time*, were confiscated or held up for weeks on end. A pall of fear descended on intellectual life in the country, but because everything was so eerily quiet, the government kept on saying that everything was normal and India was not a police state.

Of course, the Emergency was not an unmixed evil. Indira Gandhi may have been a dictator at heart and too ready to identify her own interests with those of the country. But there could be no doubt on her dedication and commitment to the welfare of her people. Apart from clamping the Emergency to seat her firmly in the saddle, she used it to lift the economy up by its bootstraps.

Immediately after proclaiming the Emergency, she announced a 20-Point Programme designed to contain inflation and provide relief to the deserving sections of the rural population and the urban middle class. This programme included items, such as ceilings on agricultural lands and distribution of the surplus among the landless, provision of house sites for farm labourers and improvement of irrigation and water supply in drought prone areas. Many of these reforms had been adopted before the Emergency, but implementation was tardy. New items included ceilings on urban property, raising of the income tax exemption limit and a moratorium on recovery of rural debt.

Then came the crackdown on smugglers, hoarders, black marketeers, tax evaders and black-money operators. Shops were told to put up a list of prices and those charging extra were penalised. Queue-jumpers at bus stops were fixed and long-haired youths had their locks trimmed. Inefficient or lazy public servants were retired or disciplined. Strikes were banned and marches and demonstrations halted.

The result was that prices came down and the annual inflation rate of 30 per cent brought to a point lower than twelve months earlier. The national income was expected to go up by five or 6 per cent in 1975–76 as compared to 2 per cent in 1974–75.

But a question to be answered was whether these gains could not have been secured by means other than the Emergency and at a lesser cost than the curtailment of fundamental freedoms. Surely, the land reforms, the tax evasion, the parallel black money economy, all these could have been dealt with if only the government had been less lackadaisical in its policy and not given the impression that it had a vested interest in corruption and big money for the winning of elections as in Uttar Pradesh.

The government blamed the delay on the obstructionist policy of the Opposition, and the legal difficulties involved in grain procurement and detention of smugglers and other racketeers. Only a change in the whole legal system and the whole Constitution, the government argued, could bring about the necessary reforms. The fundamental rights of the individual must be subjected to the collective rights of the millions. That of course sounded very much like Communist theory and so it was. Some of the men closest to the prime minister were either Communists or extreme Leftists.

Shashi Bhushan had been advocating a 'limited dictatorship' for India for a long time, with Indira as the dictator. H R Gokhale wanted a 'non-property owning democracy' in the country and the Constitution to be changed to serve the wishes of the people, of which of course the government was the sole interpreter. So they had gone to work with a will during the then current session of Parliament, doing an efficient hatchet job of wrecking the Constitution by passing 30 amendments in as many days. It was all part of the familiar Communist tactic of using the Constitution to subvert the Constitution.

The crucial question, however, was: Did Indira have a shred of evidence for imposing the Emergency? Its real purpose, as the legislation placing her election out of the purview of the courts showed, was to get her out of a jam. But the reasons then given were that the country's internal security was threatened, that a conspiracy of violence was being hatched to throw Indira out, that the Opposition parties had planned to paralyse the government by staging countrywide demonstration and strikes in front of government offices and that Jayaprakash Narayan had incited the armed forces to mutiny.

A lot of this was just eyewash. The armed forces were entirely non-political and the government had them well under control. Jayaprakash had asked them to disobey unjust orders but by no stretch of imagination to mutiny. In Bihar, it was the army and the border security police that had tried to crush the non-violent stir of Narayan's anti-corruption movement. The countrywide demonstrations were intended to force Indira Gandhi to resign by the same methods of non-violent *satyagraha* as had been used by Mahatma Gandhi to bring about an end to the British rule. Naturally there were some risks involved but nothing for which Indira invoked the Emergency.

The easiest way out of a threat to the country's security (if there was any) was for Indira to resign after the Allahabad High Court declared her election to the Parliament void. True the charges on which she was convicted were rather technical. Propriety if not legality demanded that she step down at least temporarily. Surely, in the ranks of the Congress someone could have been found to act as a caretaker till she was cleared. Instead mammoth rallies were organised and the idea spread that Indira Gandhi was indispensable. Indira was India and India was Indira.

Even so, she would perhaps not have declared the Emergency had she got another unconditional stay order from the Supreme Court. If she had, she would have continued acting as the prime minister with no restrictions, summoned the Monsoon session of the Parliament as usual, got an acquittal perhaps from the Supreme Court and then called general elections, appearing before the people as a justly aggrieved prime minister.

With only a conditional stay order how could she face the Parliament of which, according to the Allahabad High Court judgement, she was not even a member and thus could not influence the final outcome of debate? Moreover the growing unity of the Opposition parties, which had proved its worth in the Gujarat elections and the increasing momentum of Jayaprakash Narayan's movement for non-violent total revolution gave her serious cause to doubt whether she would be as successful in the 1976 elections as she had been in 1971. So she panicked and in a tremendous bid for survival cut the ground from under her enemies' feet by declaring the Emergency.

TWENTY-SEVEN

Forced Sterilisation

Population was one of Indira's and, also, the entire country's major worries. With a population of 550 million in 1974, India had 2 per cent of the world's land but 14 per cent of its people. 'We have to keep running,' said Indira, 'only to stand still.' The official government policy was that the family planning should be voluntary and no ignoble methods should be used to reduce numbers. Yet, barely six months after the declaration of Emergency, the policy was radically changed to a systematic campaign of compulsory sterilisation, which, according to Michael Henderson in *Experiment with Untruth*, caused terror throughout the land, especially in the north. People were simply bundled off into trucks and forcibly operated upon. If the entire village resisted they were simply fired upon by the police, as in Muzaffarnagar, Sultanpur and Turkman Gate. The heartlessness of Turkman Gate firing was largely due to Sanjay Gandhi, Indira's son. But did she not know? She did.

In Maharashtra, on 2 December 1975, a Bill was drafted to be introduced in the State Legislature called 'The Maharashtra Restriction of Size of Family Act 1975'. 'Every male person,' the Bill said, 'shall restrict the size of the family to not more than three living children' and if he 'has more than three... on the date of the commencement of this act shall get himself or his wife sterilised.' If he refused to do so he 'shall be liable to be punished with imprisonment for a period not exceeding six months or with fine which may extend to five hundred rupees or with both.' In the case of a government servant he shall 'be liable to be discharged from service.'

There was a storm of protest as soon as the draconian terms of the Bill came to be known. Muslims rejected it outright on religious grounds. *Sachivalaya* (Secretariat) was inundated with hundreds of lists of signatures asserting that compulsory sterilisation offended human dignity, violated consciences, was against the traditions of the country and the teachings of the Father of the Nation and was opposed to the true interests of the country. The Bill, according to the *Free Press Journal,* had stirred a hornet's nest and the chief minister had been left in no doubt that 'all sections of the population certainly do not favour it'.

In his written submission to the chief minister, Archbishop of Bombay Cardinal Valerian Gracias, who had led a delegation of Christians, pointed out that according to the UN Declaration of Human Rights the family is 'the natural and fundamental element of society, which is entitled to the protection of society and the state.' Therefore, the Cardinal argued that it were the parents who had the right to decide on the number of children, taking into account also the good of the society. Catholics agreed with the State, said the Cardinal, in its concern about the rapid population growth, but were utterly opposed to compulsory sterilisation as a means to check population increase. To force any person to undergo sterilisation or demand that a doctor or nurse perform the operation against his or her conscience, he added, was 'to ask the person to go against the divine law in his heart.' Finally, said the Cardinal, 'we as Catholics strongly object to the proposed Bill on religious grounds and we strongly resent any suggestion that our position is anti-national or based on selfish interest. We are here not precisely seeking minority rights... We claim that the move to make sterilisation compulsory would not be in the best interest of the country. In this undoubted moment of stress, let us not have recourse to means which are in the totalitarian tradition which our people repudiate.'

During the debate in the legislature, Chief Minister S B Chavan urged G M Banatwala of the Muslim League not to oppose compulsory sterilisation on religious grounds. Religion has nothing to do with this measure, said Chavan. Banatwala replied that the Bill violated the Article 25 of the Constitution and was not within the legislative competence of the house since its provisions contravened the religious tenets of Islam and Christianity. When his deputy Farokh Pasha overruled his objections, Banatwala called for a poll. Strangely, 75 members supported the motion. Banatwala, the lone warrior, opposed it.

At the Centre, Union Health Minister Karan Singh issued a national policy statement on 16 April 1976. Rejecting central legislation for compulsory sterilisation, the statement said, 'the administrative and medical infrastructure in many parts of the country is still inadequate to cope with the vast implications of nationwide compulsory sterilisation. 'Where however,' the statement added, 'a state legislature... decides that the time is ripe and it is necessary to pass legislation for compulsory sterilisation it may do so.'

During the debate in the Lok Sabha, the majority of speakers especially women, were opposed to compulsory sterilisation. Karan

Singh made it clear that the Centre was not for any pressure or harassment in implementing the Family Planning programme.

Maharashtra obviously thought the time was ripe. S B Chavan told a Press conference that he was going ahead with his plans, no matter what the Opposition said. To dispose of the spate of memorandum that kept pouring into the state secretariat, a Joint Select Committee of 27 members, headed by K M Patil, was appointed. It was to study the memoranda and interview people who wanted to present their views. Whether the committee considered these memoranda seriously or not, it proposed that any person who refused to be sterilised after his third child would be put in jail and 'be liable to be forcibly sterilised and have the pregnancy terminated.'

In the event, in spite of the objections of Banatwala and three dissenting members of the Joint Select Committee, the Compulsory Sterilisation Bill, now called the Restriction of Family Size Bill was passed. From the time the Bill was introduced four months earlier, the mind of the state government seemed to have been made up. The initiative, in fact, seemed to have come from the Centre. Clear indication of this was given by the prime minister when she said that some of the rights of the individual must give place to the rights of the nation, the right to live, to progress. It was all part of the Emergency mindset. The national policy statement on population, however, apart from the section on forced sterilisation, was an admirable document, reflecting some of the best and most advanced thinking on population. Population policy, it said, must be seen as part of an integral strategy of development, seeking to improve the quality of life in the country. The real enemy is poverty and without a medium of economic development no real cultural or spiritual progress can be made.

Hence, the need for a global assault on ignorance, illiteracy, superstition and disease that are the breeding grounds of poverty.

Simply to wait for education and development to bring about a drop in fertility is not a practical solution. The population problem does exist and in crisis proportion. With an increase of one million people per month, the population explosion has largely diluted the fruits of the remarkable economic progress we have made over the last two decades.'

The national policy statement made as its goal the reduction of the birth rate from 35 per thousand at the beginning of the Fifth Five-Year Plan to 25 per thousand at the end of the Sixth Five-Year Plan. Allowing for a steady decline in the death rate, the growth rate of the population would be down to 1.4 per cent. The effective means for achieving this target were: raising the minimum age of marriage to 18 for girls and 21 for boys, improvement in the level of female education for girls and non-formal education, introduction of population values in the educational system and child nutrition programmes.

TWENTY-EIGHT

Remaking the Constitution

Compulsory sterilisation could have been excused as an extreme measure devised to fight an extremely difficult problem. But what could not be pardoned was the overt attempt to use Parliament to subvert democracy and the Constitution. The 44th Constitution Amendment Act passed at the end of 1976 was not just a tinkering with the periphery of India's foundational document, but a radical move to alter its basic structure, concentrating all power in the prime minister. It was a remaking of the Constitution.

The sinister design was evident from the start. Our founding fathers had written a Preamble to the Constitution, which said that India was a sovereign democratic republic. The 44th amendment stated that the Preamble should now be read as 'a sovereign, secular, socialist and democratic republic.'

In an article in the *Illustrated Weekly of India* the noted jurist, Nani A Palkhiwala, showed that the Preamble to the Constitution is a Preamble and not the Constitution itself. Parliament may have the power to amend the Constitution. It does not have the power to amend the Preamble to the Constitution.

'The Preamble,' Palkhivala wrote, 'from its very nature, is incapable of being amended. It refers to the most momentous event in India's history and sets out, as a matter of historical fact, what the people of India resolved in 1949 to do for their unfolding future. No Parliament can amend or alter this historical past.'

What gave the whole game away was that this Act gave Parliament unrestricted power to amend the Constitution and stated that any legislation it carried out in pursuance of the Constitution's Directive Principles of State Policy, could not be challenged on the ground that it violated any of the fundamental rights, except those conferred on minorities.

The legislative powers of Parliament were thus put beyond judicial review and Parliament became the supreme authority in the land. The consequence was, wrote Palkhivala, that the rights to life and personal liberty, the freedom to form associations and assemble peacefully, the right to move freely throughout the country and the right to equality before the law would virtually stand abrogated. The chapter of Fundamental Rights belongs to the basic structure of the Constitution and if these rights could be abrogated, then that basic structure would be destroyed.

'The idea that the rights could be amended or abridged' wrote K Santhanam, who was a member of the Constituent Assembly, that formed the Constitution, 'never entered the mind of anyone in the Assembly... The recent claim of the ruling party that the Directive Principles are more important than the Fundamental Rights and the latter may be restricted or superseded in trying to implement the former was altogether opposed to the intention of the Constituent Assembly.'

It was 'We the People' who gave us the Constitution to protect our rights even against Parliament, which we ourselves had chosen, if it went beyond the mandate that we gave it for its five-year term of office.

The dangerous implications of the amendment to the Article 368 of the Constitution by the 44th Amendment Act 1976, taking away the power of the Judiciary to question the validity of any amendment of the Constitution by Parliament, were clearly seen when read together with the amendment to the Article 31C.

As it stood, said Constitution expert M C Chagla, at a meeting of Citizens for Democracy, the Article 31C permitted legislatures to pass any law in violation of Fundamental Rights, provided it was for the purposes of implementing the Directive Principles. Now Parliament and State Legislatures can pass any law in violation of fundamental rights for the ostensible purpose of implementing Directive Principles and it cannot be challenged in court, it is not justiciable. The Directive Principles have taken precedence over Fundamental Rights. 'The underlying fallacy of this Bill,' said M C Chagla,' is that Parliament is sovereign. It is not. It is the people who are sovereign. As things stand today, if you increase the power of Parliament, you are increasing the power of the government, the cabinet and in effect of the PM.'

The 44th Amendment of the Constitution Bill was introduced in the Lok Sabha on 1 September 1976 and came up for discussion when Parliament met on 25 October 1976. Earlier, a committee under Swaran Singh had been set up to make proposals for changes in the Constitution and discuss them with leaders of the Opposition parties.

The prime minister had called for a debate before the Constitution was amended. But in an emergency, a debate was not really possible and the response was meagre. When Parliament met at the end of 1976, it was taken for granted that the Bill would be passed by the ruling party's steamroller majority. And so it was. The Bill became the 44th Constitution Amendment Act. A structural change was brought about in the country's Constitution and the delicate balance between the judiciary, the executive and the legislature considerably altered. The country became monolithic, concentrating all powers in the prime minister.

Other amendments made the President of India completely subservient to the prime minister, extended the life of Parliament from five to six years and drastically curtailed the powers of the judiciary. Once Parliament or the State Legislative had passed a law, it was almost impossible for the court to set it aside.

TWENTY-NINE

Indira Springs a Surprise

The 44th Amendment to the Constitution Amendment Act concentrated all the powers in the prime minister's hands, extending the life of Parliament for a year with provision that it could be extended still further. Hence, the Emergency was firmly in place. It might have been thought that now at least Indira would give all her attention to carrying out her 20-Point Programme to bring about a change in the quality of life of her people.

Why then did Indira Gandhi change tack mid-course and sprung a surprise on the nation and the world by calling for general elections? Could it be that she had yielded to pressure from President of the United States James Earl 'Jimmy' Carter, Jr or the World Bank that wanted India to return to democracy ? Or, was it that she did not want Zulfikar Ali Bhutto who had announced elections in Pakistan, to steal a march on her? Or, was it that she felt that 19 months were altogether too long a period to keep thousands of people in jail without trial, among whom were prominent people such as Morarji Desai and Ashoka Mehta? Or, was it that rumblings within the Congress were getting so loud that the cracks had begun to surface and threatened to break up the organisation?

Whatever the reasons, the calling of elections and the relaxation of Emergency meant India's return, however brief, to democracy. It put new heart into those who had despaired of Indian democracy but were now determined to put it back on the rails, cost what it may. In the last analysis, elections are what democracy is all about. 'Our system,' said Indira in a broadcast, 'rests on the belief that governments derive their power from the people and that the people give expression to their sovereign will freely and without hindrance by choosing the government they want and by indicating their preferences for policies.'

Implicit in Indira's statement was that the elections would be free and fair. But would they be so? For one thing, the Emergency had only been relaxed, not withdrawn. Political meetings were now permitted, but the right to lawful assembly and freedom of expression and movement still remained suspended.

The Maintenance of Internal Security Act (MISA) was still there to clap anyone whom the government thought undesirable into jail without trial. Press censorship had been lifted, but newspapers still had to look over their shoulders lest they got into trouble with the Publication of Objectionable Matters Act and the Code of Journalistic Ethics.

In any case, it was only one or two big newspapers that were truly independent; the rest were government controlled if not government owned. *Samachar* (News), which was formed by the merger of four news agencies, was the only news agency to give the official version. The All India Radio and television peddled government propaganda.

More serious was the time allotted before the elections. Two months was altogether too short for the opposition parties to gather their forces, collect funds and get their electioneering off the ground. While the Congress and the Communist Party of India (CPI) had their organisations geared for any eventuality, the leaders of the opposition and thousands of their rank and file had been languishing in jail without the benefit of a trial. What the total number of political prisoners was had never been disclosed.

Home Minister Brahamananda Reddy once said that two out of every lakh of population were in jail. This must have been a gross underestimate since even three weeks after orders had been given for their release, Opposition leaders were complaining that 10 thousand of their party members were still in jail. In fact, fairly reliable estimates put the figure at nothing less than two lakh.

Obviously, state governments were dragging their feet in releasing the prisoners so that the Opposition parties would be unable to organise their cadres for the election campaign.

As for funds, the Congress had enormous resources and good friends among big industrialists; whereas the few industrialists who were sympathetic to the Opposition dared not stick their necks out.

The dice was heavily loaded against the Opposition. As the Opposition leaders came out of jail one by one, they painted a grim picture of what they went through. Some of the prisoners, they said, had died in jail, and others tortured. All had endured severe hardships. The police picked many of them without being given any reason. They had lost their jobs and left their families in distress. Eighty-year-old former Dy Prime Minister Morarji Desai had been isolated in a room for a month and after that allowed to go for a walk only once a day and that too after dark in a scorpion and snake infested compound.

Jayaprakash Narayan, who had given his name to the JP Movement in Bihar, had been released earlier, but only because the government did not want his death on their hands. All these harrowing tales evoked immense sympathy from the huge rallies they addressed in Delhi and other cities.

Adversity had made strange bedfellows of the opposition leaders. Shared suffering made such disparate parties as the old Congress, the Jana Sangh, the Rightist Bharatiya Lok Dal and the Socialists shed their identity and come together on the common platform of the Janata Party, which they formed with Morarji Desai as the chairman and party's common symbol chosen was that of a man and a plough.

Their manifesto was a powerful indictment of the 19 months of the Emergency. The choice before the country, they said, was between freedom and slavery, democracy and dictatorship. The 44th Constitution Amendment Act of 1978, that had been bull-dozed through Parliament concentrated all power in the hands of the prime minister, subverted the basic structure of the 1950s Constitution, vitiated the federal principle and upset the balance between the people and Parliament, Parliament and the judiciary and the executive. The question before the electorate was—could the Emergency take the credit for whatever was achieved during the period between 1975–1977 and was the price the country had to pay in terms of freedom and human rights necessary or commensurate with the supposed gains.

The manifesto went on to show that these gains were largely illusory. Prices had increased by 12 per cent in the past eleven months and unemployement by 1.5 million. It mounted a fierce attack on the policy of forced sterilisation. 'Panic and anger,' it said, 'have culminated in resort to firing and terror. Unsuspecting and ineligible persons have been herded and forcibly taken to sterilisation camps. Human dignity has been set at naught by these indefensible actions. The Janata Party instituted an inquiry into allegations of excesses.'

But the manifesto was not just negative. It went on to sketch outlines of a new society that should take the place of the existing one if India was to break out of the vicious circle of the few rich getting richer while the great masses of the poor getting poorer still. At that time, said the manifesto, 70 per cent of the people of India were below the poverty line. A quarter century of planning had failed to provide for the masses the six basic necessities of life: Food, safe drinking water, clothing, housing, education and healthcare—116,000 villages were without facilities for drinking water. 'There cannot be two societies, rich and poor,' said the manifesto, 'the latter subserving the goals of elitism, urbanism and consumerism.' 'The Janata Party will level down as much as level up and redistribute income and wealth to build a just society. It will establish an economy in which agriculture, cottage and small industries have primacy and are not sacrificed for the big machine and the big city. It will reorient goals and priorities to adopt a pattern of development that answers our needs to find full employment and better life for our people and to stay clear of the evils of capitalist and totalitarian industrialisation.'

'It will shift the emphasis to labour-intensive technologies and the production of mass consumption goods. Rural-urban disparities will be narrowed down and a rural-urban nexus will prevent the growth of mega cities and slum cities. Political power will be decentralised by giving greater responsibility to local bodies like municipalities and village *panchayats.*'

That the Opposition parties could unite came perhaps as a surprise to Indira. They had done so before in 1971 and she dismissed them as a mish-mash and a hotchpotch of conflicting ideologies.

What shocked her was the resignation of Food Minister Jagjivan Ram from the Congress and his decision to form a rival party, the Congress for Democracy (CFD), together with Nandini Sathpathy, former chief minister of Orissa and Hemvati Nandan Bahuguna, former chief minister of Uttar Pradesh. Jagjivan Ram had been one of the stalwarts of the Congress for over 30 years. He had stood by her during the split in 1969 and with his support she was assured of getting the votes of Dalits, who formed 15 per cent of the electorate. What was worse was that Jagjivan Ram's resignation brought to the surface the cracks in the Congress organisation. He accused her of taking the country towards a dictatorship. She alone took decisions, like the imposition of the Emergency and the holding of elections, without consulting the Cabinet. They were only informed. Chief ministers who commanded comfortable majority in their state legislatures were unceremoniously dismissed and her own favourites put in their places. Even the list of candidates for the elections had to be approved by her personally. 'Government wants to sustain itself, perpetuate itself,' said Jagjivan Ram, 'by measures like the Emergency and the extraordinary law... A fear psychosis has overtaken the whole nation.'

Jagjivan Ram charged the prime minister with setting up 'extra constitutional centres of power.' The state machinery was being used to boost an individual, who made policy statements even though he had no official status. He was referring to Sanjay Gandhi, the prime minister's son, whom she was grooming as her successor. He was hopping from state capital to state capital, ordering top Congress leaders like Siddartha Shankar Ray, the chief minister of West Bengal, to organise huge rallies for him to address on the three topics—family planning, slum clearance and dowry. Indeed, Sanjay Gandhi's enthusiasm for forced sterilisation had been such that riots had broken out in Delhi and people had been killed in the police firing. So greatly had the Muslims of Delhi been alienated that the Imam of Jama Masjid came to have talks with Jagjivan Ram when he formed his rival party. Sanjay Gandhi was going round the country ostensibly to strengthen the Youth Congress and inject new blood into the party. For the 540 seats in the Lok Sabha, the Youth Congress hoped to get at least 250 in the list of the Congress candidates. After Jagjivan Ram's exit, the number dropped to less than 50. Sanjay Gandhi faded out for some time from the public eye and sitting members who were to be displaced got their seats again. Sanjay Gandhi stood for elections from the Amethi constituency, next to that of his mother, Rai Bareili, where she was again being opposed by Socialist leader Raj Narain who filed the suit against her in the Allahabad High Court for corrupt electoral practices.

The exodus from the Congress that was expected in the wake of Jagjivan Ram's resignation did not take place. Indira Gandhi acted swiftly and got the other top Congress leaders to pledge their loyalty to her. But a sizeable number joined him together with the Young Turks and others who had left the Congress earlier. Jagjivan Ram Congress for Democracy now entered into an electoral adjustment with the Janata Party and fought the election on the same symbol.

Indira was upset. She said the people 'can go to hell' if they went along with the Opposition parties. A worse shock for her was the decision of her aunt Vijayalakshmi Pandit, Jawaharlal Nehru's sister and former president of the UN General Assembly, to come out into the open and support Jagjivan Ram. Vijayalakshmi had said there were reasons for the proclamation of the Emergency since the country had been taken so far away from the ideals for which they had fought before Independence that her conscience would not let her remain quiet. Democratic institutions that had been built up through the years after Independence were smothered and destroyed one after another.

On her part, Indira was going to the polls with the record of her party's performance, especially on the economic front and promising them stability and progress. The Congress manifesto let the statistics speak. Inflation had been successfully combated. The price level was lower than in October 1974. Food production in 1976 reached an all-time high of 120 million tonnes, the growth rate of industrial production rose to 5.7 per cent and the gross national income went up by more than 6.5 per cent. The balance of payments (BoP) position was comfortable, an excellent export performance leading up to a record accumulation of over Rs 2,500 crore in foreign exchange reserves.

Congress took the credit for the steps taken under the 20-Point Programme to carry out land reforms, distribute house sites, liquidate rural indebtedness, abolish bonded labour, enforce minimum wages for agricultural labourers and improve the condition of farm workers. On the basis of this performance, the government promised to go ahead with its programme with greater vigour to maintain the closest vigil on prices, to launch a national housing fund, to establish an agricultural development bank of India, to spread literacy to all citizens and in general to pursue the policies it had followed over the years for increased production and greater social justice.

The manifesto defended the 42nd Constitutional Amendment Act of 1976 that inserted important words like 'Socialist' and 'Secular' in the Preamble as being necessary to carry out social reforms, and the imposition of Emergency as required to save the country from violence and chaos. It said the Congress was pledged to defend the rights of minorities, especially the right to manage and administer educational institutions of their choice. Finally, in a sudden volte-face it categorically stated there could not and would not 'be any compulsion in the family planning programme.

THIRTY

A Monumental Blunder

The calling of elections proved to be a monumental blunder. The whole country was seething with discontent and as on 16 March 1977 news of the Congress defeat came pouring in on the scoreboards and over the air, the mood was reminiscent of nothing so much as the coming of Independence. Jubilation all around, crackers were fired in celebrations. The slogan of *Janata Party Zindabad* rent the air. People slept with transistors glued to their ears. At three in the morning, they strolled from room to room breaking the news; the prime minister had lost. After 21 months, the country awoke to a new dawn of freedom and the pall of fear was lifted.

One clear conclusion emerged from the results. The Congress was routed and that was because of the Emergency. In the four states of the country, Uttar Pradesh, Bihar, Punjab and Haryana, the Congress did not get even a single seat. Indira and her son were defeated. This was a proof of massive revulsion from all that the

Congress stood for and the people were in no mood to give her another five years of authoritarian rule.

In almost every instance the Congress candidate lost by a hundred thousand votes, sometimes by two or three hundred thousand.

The Janata hurricane, therefore, made a clean sweep, especially in the north. South of the Vindhyas, however, the sweep was less clear. In the north, the Emergency had touched the lives of almost every individual, in the south local issues like the pro- and anti-DMK and the fairly good record of the ruling coalition in Kerala were more predominant.

In the north, the Janata hurricane made a clean sweep because people had seen or at least heard of men and women being picked up by the police and thrown into jail without a trial, being bundled off into trucks and forcibly sterilised and when they resisted being fired on by the police.

In her whirlwind tour, the prime minister had put the blame for what she called the few stray cases on overzealous officials. People listened but did not believe her. She had lost credibility, as had her son Sanjay Gandhi, Bansilal, Vidya Charan Shukla and H R Gokhale. They suffered in silence, but when opportunity came took their revenge and humbled their oppressors. There could have been no more pathetic figure than Bansilal praying for forgiveness and the people's votes. Alas, it was too late.

Straight from jail, on the other hand, the Janata Party candidates, at least many of them, had only to appear before one of those huge spontaneous rallies and immediately strike a chord of sympathy in the hearts of the electorate. The harrowing tales they told of their sufferings in jail placed on their heads a halo of martyrdom. The hearts of the electorate went out to them and they gave them freely the votes they wanted.

The elections also showed that India was not only the largest democracy in the world but also had reached within thirty years a maturity that would have done credit to a much older democracy. Given a clear option, the electorate showed it could make up its mind and arrive at a rational decision.

The US President Jimmy Carter rightly drew the attention of the world to the fact that India had proved herself to be a true democracy by bringing about a change in government without violence or revolution and was, therefore, an example to the world.

Finally, credit must be given to Indira, who whatever her motives, called for elections, allowed them to run their course and finally bowed to their verdict. In this, she showed herself to be a true democrat. 'My colleagues and I,' she said, 'accept the verdict unreservedly and in a spirit of humility.'

THIRTY-ONE

Democracy Back on Track

In New Delhi, the new ministers moved into the spacious bungalows left by the Raj. Like Mughals, the British and the Congress held court while sycophants and turncoats waited on their pleasure. Files piled up in the secretariats, but a few decisions were taken. A hundred days after the general elections swept the Janata Party into power, there were a few signs of the radical transformation that was expected.

The Janata Party had come to power in a burst of moral fervour. But for all their high-sounding principles, their pledge to put service before self and to give the country a clean and honest administration, between the idea and the reality fell the shadow. Barely had the ink dried on the voting slips, feathers were ruffled over the prime ministership.

The choice of prime minister, it had been understood, would be made democratically. Instead, it was changed to consensus and when this looked like going in favour of Janata Party chairman Morarji

Desai, Jagjivan Ram, leader of the Congress for Democracy (CFD), took umbrage. Together with George Fernandes and Raj Narain, he failed to turn up when the new Cabinet took the oath of office. Matters became worse when Charan Singh was made the home minister and it looked as though Jagjivan would not be even No. 2. It was only when Jayaprakash Narayan, the country's moral leader, assured him that he would always be No. 2 whatever his portfolio, that his hurt feelings were assuaged.

Jagjivan Ram joined the Cabinet but continued to sulk. His CFD had fought the elections under the Janata Party's symbol on the understanding that after the elections, the two parties would merge. But with the defeat of Indira, there arose the likelihood of a large-scale exodus from the Congress into the CFD and a strengthening of Jagjivan Ram's bargaining position vis-a-vis the Janata Party.

So, he refused to merge. The CFD, he said, had still 'a vital role to play in the consolidation of democratic forces.' In other words, he was keeping the doors open for defection. But if there was one political game, which those who had voted for the Janata believed was over and done with, it was floor crossing or defection. Indira played it unashamedly bringing down several state governments and the Janata Party had condemned her soundly for it. So the CFD's decision not to merge provoked a hostile reaction.

Fortunately, wiser counsels prevailed and when on 1 May 1977, the Janata Party met to finalise the merger of its constituents, Jagjivan Ram was there to add to the general jubilation.

The problem of defection, however, continued to plague the Janata Party. In its manifesto, it promised to introduce an Anti-defection Bill. It found that unless it admitted defectors, its strength would be permanently reduced. It had no countrywide organisation.

The Congress with its overwhelming majority in the Rajya Sabha and the state assemblies could effectively obstruct any legislation that the Janata Party might introduce in accordance with its manifesto that required the approval of these bodies. In fact, when the Janata Party introduced a Bill to repeal the 42nd Constitution Amendment Act that had made Indira virtually a dictator, the Bill was hastily withdrawn since the Congress refused to support it.

Moreover, the Presidential election was due in August 1977. Unless the Janata Party had a majority in the Rajya Sabha and the state assemblies, an anti-Janata candidate, even a person like Indira could be appointed, thus creating complications. So, the Janata Party sacrificed principles to real politics and decided to welcome into the fold, unconditionally and indiscriminately, members from the other parties.

The Presidential election led the Janata Party to embark on a venture that tarnished its image still further. As hopes of large-scale defection from among the Congress members of the Rajya Sabha and state assemblies began to dwindle. The Janata leaders thought that their best bet for securing a president of their choice was to dissolve the assemblies in the nine states where the Congress had been routed in the general elections. But, according to the amended Constitution, there was no precedent for dissolving a state assembly just because its majority party had lost in the general elections.

India's Constitution is federal, dividing powers between the Centre and the states. Rejection of a party at the Centre did not mean its rejection in the state. When Indira had dissolved the Tamil Nadu state assembly, even though the DMK members still commanded an overwhelming majority, she was rightly criticised.

Now the Janata Party wanted to do just what it had condemned. Its constitutional experts quoted Dicey and Halisbury. The sovereign, they said, had the right to dismiss a government that had forfeited the confidence of the electorate.

Since in the nine states, it was the chief ministers and their cabinets who had carried out the repressive measures of the Emergency, against which the people had voted, they had to go. The life of these parties had besides been unlawfully prolonged by a parliament that had outrun its mandate.

Morally, therefore, the decision to dissolve the assemblies seemed to be correct, constitutionally the matter was unclear. When its own interests were at stake, the Janata Party, usually such a stickler for constitutional propriety, threw it to the winds.

But the Janata Party's troubles were not over. No sooner had the acting president B D Jatti ruled that the assemblies were dissolved and fresh elections could now be held in Tamil Nadu and the nine states, than the scramble for tickets began. Never before had so many candidates for the state elections applied for tickets from a single party. For three thousand seats there were 25 thousand applicants and Chandrasekhar, the president of the Janata Party, had the unenviable task of choosing those who were the most worthy to represent the party.

The scramble for tickets brought to the surface the deep division within the Janata Party. Shared suffering in jail had brought together the leaders of the old Congress, the Bharatiya Lok Dal (BLD), the Jana Sangh and the Socialists.

During their election campaign when critics asked how such disparate elements could hold together, they constantly replied that they had burnt their bridges and renounced their former identities.

On 1 May 1977, the four parties had officially wound up, leaving only the Janata Party in existence. But group loyalties and traditional loyalties die hard and as soon as the state elections were announced, they reemerged to corner as large a share of the party nominations as they could. For all these reasons a faint mood of disenchantment with the Janata Party seemed to have crept in.

The results of the state elections, however, clearly showed that the Janata wave was not weakening. In Haryana, Uttar Pradesh, Orissa, Madhya Pradesh, Bihar, Himachal Pradesh and Rajasthan, the party won a two-thirds majority. In the Punjab, together with its allies, it swept the polls. Although in West Bengal and Tamil Nadu, it lost to the Marxists and the DMK respectively, on the whole its spectacular success at the national level was repeated now at the state level.

Conspicuous in the state election results was the complete rout of the Congress. The party that had ruled the country for over 30 years and considered the Opposition an irrelevance was reduced to an insignificant rump, destined for extinction.

For this shameful defeat, it had only itself to blame. It knew the people had turned against it for the repressive measures of the Emergency: the demolition of poor people's homes, the enforced sterilisation that led to 150 deaths in Madhya Pradesh alone, the firing on crowds that resisted the sterilisation measures, the imprisonment without trial of thousands, the gruesome methods of torture, the lying propaganda, the hubris of Sanjay Gandhi, Bansilal and company.

Instead of making a clean breast of it, the Congress blamed its defeat in the general elections not on the Emergency, but only its excesses. It clung to the former leadership and the caucus around it, choosing Brahmananda Reddy as president and let Indira do the backseat driving. She remained unrepentant, blaming the defeat on bad timing.

The lingering revulsion for the Congress, however, did not account wholly for the Janata Party's victory in the state elections. Part of the credit was due to the Janata Party itself, which with all its faults had shouldered the heavy burden of clearing away the debris of the Emergency and the many years of Congress misrule.

In keeping with the pledge it took at Mahatma Gandhi's *samadhi* to uphold the right to life and liberty of all citizens, it had begun dismantling the structures of fear and repression built during the previous regime. It had repealed the Prevention of Publication of Objectionable Matters Act and restored to the press its immunity in reporting parliamentary proceedings. It had allowed Opposition leaders like Y B

Chavan to appear on radio and television and criticise the government, even to campaign for their parties before the elections. It had restored fundamental freedoms and the judiciary to its rightful place. Democracy was back on track and India's foreign relations were excellent.

In its manifesto, the Janata Party had promised to give the country bread and freedom and build the new society. The new budget made a beginning in the fulfilment of these promises. Development outlay was stepped up and a major share, namely 30.4 per cent, earmarked for agriculture and allied services, including irrigation and power for rural areas. There was provision for durable link roads in rural areas and rural water supply. Small-scale and village industries were given concessions and facilities provided for sound industrial units to take over the sick ones. Defence and non-plan expenditure were cut down and deficit financing reduced to Rs 76 crore, the lowest in many years.

Despite this, inflation was mounting at the rate of about 14 per cent, several essential goods were in short supply and their prices had risen sharply. Unemployment was increasing and the budget made no attempt to map out a full employment strategy.

On 7 July 1977, the Janata Party and the Congress agreed to support the candidacy of Neelam Sanjiva Reddy, speaker of the Lok Sabha, in the Presidential elections and on 6 August 1977, Sanjiva Reddy was sworn in as India's new President. With the state elections behind it and the new President elected, the new Janata government was now expected to put its shoulders more firmly to the wheel of economic development. It had acquired an enormous fund of goodwill and it was hoped it would not squander it as the Congress had done.

THIRTY-TWO

Janata on the Decline

One year after the general elections had swept the Janata Party into power, some more assembly elections showed it could not be categorised simply as a party of the north. In Maharashtra and Assam, it emerged as the largest party and in Andhra Pradesh and Karnataka as the second largest. In Andhra and Karnataka, Congress (I) won absolute majority and could not, therefore, be written off as a party of no consequence.

News of the Shah Commission, which made inquiries into the excessess committed during the Emergency, had apparently not percolated down to the south and large crowds welcomed Indira wherever she went.

Posing as the champion of the Dalits and the oppressed, she swung the votes in her favour. But it was in Azamgarh, Uttar Pradesh, that the parliamentary by-elections showed the tide was slowly but surely turning back. In this prestigious constituency, which had returned the UP Chief Minister Ram Naresh Yadav, a Janata Party candidate, the Congress candidate won with a comfortable majority.

Uttar Pradesh was the heart of the Hindi heartland and Indira's return to her home state, from where she had been so unceremoniously routed, seemed to show the memories of the Emergency's excesses were slowly fading away.

On the other hand, Azamgarh could also have been a portent that the Janata tide had begun to recede. All that the masses now saw was the squabbling in the UP Janata Party. In UP, the infighting had reached a crucial stage because of the dismissal by Narendra Jadhav, a senior minister. Similar internecine fighting was also witnessed in Bihar, where Janata Party dissidents called for the dismissal of the Bharatiya Lok Dal (BLD) chief minister Devi Lal. They charged the chief minister with maladministration and forced him to seek a vote of confidence.

The infighting at the state level was a reflection of the infighting at the national level, where the BLD Home Minister Charan Singh saw Devi Lal's difficulties as an attack on himself engineered by Chandrasekhar and Krishan Kant, two other top Janata Party leaders. Charan Singh accused them of trying to establish their own support base in Haryana at the expense of the BLD. Charan Singh looked on Devi Lal's case also as a trial of strength between himself and Jagjivan Ram, the Janata Party president. Charan Singh represented the tough and land owning Jat peasantry while Jagjivan was the leader of the Dalits. Caste rather than class was at the bottom of most of the violence that plagued the country and Charan Singh resented the BLD being blamed for the deterioration in the law and order situation.

Indeed, the squabbling had now reached the highest level. Charan Singh alleged that Prime Minister Morarji Desai and others in the Cabinet were being soft on Indira and not setting up a special court to try her. She, he said, should be arrested as soon as possible. Earlier, he raised a talk of corruption at higher places and demanded an inquiry into charges against Kanti Desai, the prime minister's son. Whereupon the prime minister, having been given a carte blanche to take Charan Singh's statement as a breach of party discipline and collective cabinet responsibility, ordered his resignation as home minister.

The consequences of that move were fatal. Charan Singh replied that it was not his statement on Indira, but his demand for an inquiry into the prime minister's son that had made him call for his resignation. The Kanti affair, thus, burst upon the country and the work of Parliament was brought to a halt by the interminable wrangling over it. Indira made a political capital out of it and ministers threatened to resign, as the prime minister would not agree to an inquiry.

Then came the massive Kisan Rally in Delhi on Charan Singh's birthday. It showed how great was his clout in north India and the danger to the survival of democracy in India if the BLD were to split from the Janata Party.

The prime minister had no option but to forgo an apology from him over the Kanti affair. He brought him back as deputy prime minister and gave him an additional charge of finance ministry.

Jayaprakash Narayan and Ram Joshi impressed upon Morarji Desai and Charan Singh that everything that had been gained by the formation of the Janata Party would be lost if they continued with their endless personal animosities and confrontation.

The Janata Party was, thus, staggering from crisis to crisis, always on the point of breaking up but at the last minute papering over the cracks with a compromise. It was believed to muddle through till the 1982 elections fearing the return of Indira. But in July 1979, six months later, the ground seemed to give way visibly under its feet and the end came so suddenly that most commentators were caught unawares. A set of circumstances combined to bring about its untimely end.

For one thing, Indira's spectre seemed to have been suddenly removed. One of her trusted lieutenants, Devaraj Urs, the chief minister of Karnataka, resenting her unrelenting advocacy of her son Sanjay. Her constant interference in the state's affairs raised the banner of revolt. He called a convention of all Congressmen and resolved to unify the party minus Indira.

For another, Morarji's calling in the army to suppress the countrywide strike of the Central Reserve Police Force (CRPF) and the pitched battles fought between them that left 30 men dead and hundreds injured showed conclusively that something was tragically wrong and that the government had lost control.

The CRPF were agitating for the redressal of their grievances. So, at the bottom, the trouble was partly economic. Indeed, the whole country was plagued with labour unrest, transport bottlenecks and shortage of coal and power. Prices were rising ominously and the estimate was that the rate of inflation would double after a few months to 17 per cent. Then there was the almost total breakdown of law and order. Communal riots broke out in several parts of the country. In Jamshedpur, India's steel city, and in Aligarh, site of the Muslim University, Hindu-Muslim riots resulted in the loss of hundreds of lives and burning down of entire areas. Similar tales of loot, arson and rape were reported from several towns as a result of riots between Dalits and caste Hindus.

In the midst of it all, the unflappable Morarji Desai remained completely unruffled, a symbol of monumental smugness. The crisis, he told journalists, was in their heads, not in reality. So long as he had the Jana Sangh with him, he had no cause for fear and he would stand solidly by the Jana Sangh because the Jana Sangh has stood solidly by him over the Kanti affair.

It was this close identification of the prime minister with the Jana Sangh and the growing power of the RSS, its militant Hindu revivalist core, that was one of the major causes of the Janata Party falling apart. With its strong grassroots base, the Jana Sangh had undoubtedly been one of the causes of the Janata Party's victory in the elections, but its links with the RSS, were believed to be one of the major stumbling blocks in the formation of the Janata Party. Not until O P Tyagi, its acting secretary, gave assurance that the RSS stood disbanded if others agreed to join hands with the Jana Sangh.

But the RSS remained very much alive and with its influence succeeded in capturing for the Jana Sangh all the key positions in the Janata Party organisation. It was the RSS that was alleged to be at the bottom of the Hindu-Muslim riots in Jamshedpur and Aligarh and the troubles in the sensitive northeastern part of India. Even such apparently good secularists, like Atal Behari Vajpayee and L K Advani, eventually showed that they were protagonists of a Hindu *rashtra*. Then, the prime minister's own fads such as Prohibition, Hindi, the banning of cow slaughter and anti-conversion coincided well with the interests of the RSS and the Jana Sangh. Every time the issue of dual membership (that Janata Party members could not belong to the RSS) came up, it was effectively scotched with the help of the prime minister. Finally, it was the successful toppling of the BLD chief ministers of Haryana, Uttar Pradesh and Bihar that convinced the BLD that conspiracy was afoot to oust Charan Singh from his post. Raj Narain, the maverick health minister, charged that the Janata Party president Chandrasekhar was with the Jana Sangh for this purpose.

Just at that time, the Monsoon session of Parliament was approaching and Y B Chavan, leader of the Opposition, was to move a vote of no-confidence against the government. Raj Narain seized the opportunity, resigned from the Janata Party, and when the session opened, sat in the Opposition benches.

A veritable landslide followed. Within three or four days, a hundred parliamentarians left the Janata Party, including several Cabinet ministers such as George Fernandes and H Bahuguna, mainly on the grounds that the Janata Party had betrayed the country's tradition of a secular democracy and alienated the minorities. The crucial vote was to come up on Monday, 16 July 1977. Late on Sunday evening, the prime minister realised the game was up. He drove to the Rashtrapati Bhavan and submitted his resignation to the President.

THIRTY-THREE

Janata's Fall

The resignation of Morarji Desai as prime minister led to a chaotic state of affairs. The frantic search for a successor government was proving to be increasingly futile. The different parties were all in disarray, having split and split again. Negotiations between them for the choice of a new prime minister yielded no results. Horse-trading on a colossal scale and a toppling game was now being witnessed at the Centre. It was all a game of numbers.

Charan Singh had accused Morarji Desai of dragging his feet in the matter of putting Indira Gandhi under arrest, but he was ready to accept help from Indira Gandhi. He left the Janata Party after Morarji Desai resigned and he took up the leaderships of the Janata (S), which his trusty lieutenant, Raj Narain, had started when he went and sat in the Opposition benches. Charan Singh could count over 90 MPs on his side and probably with the help of the two Congresses, the Left parties and others, he told President Sanjiva Reddy, that he could form a viable government. On the other hand, the Janata Party was still the single largest party in Parliament. Morarji Desai had not resigned from the leadership of this party and so he staked his claim to be called by the President to form the government, even though constitutional experts argued that his claim was anomalous. Defence Minister Jagjivan Ram and the Janata Party as a whole tried to put pressure on Morari Desai to resign as party president. But to no avail. Desai could not be moved. A meeting of the Janata Parliamentary Party had hoped to persuade Desai to resign but had to be called off. His friends, the Jana Sangh, stated they would stand by Morarji Desai and would not ask him to resign unless he did so of his own will.

Within the Janata Party, consensus seemed to be building around Jagjivan Ram as successor to Morarji Desai, the former claiming the support of 218 members of Parliament besides support from other parties. Averse to Charan Singh, Jagjivan Ram was projected as having an edge over Charan Singh.

As leader of India's 150 million Dalits and tribals, he would have considerable clout. But Morarji Desai clung to the leadership of the party and Jagjivan Ram's chances were blocked. Jagjivan Ram and Chandrasekhar went to see the President, but did not produce a list showing that the Janata Party could command a majority in the house as Indira Gandhi's Congress would not support Jagjivan Ram.

It became evident to President Neelam Sanjiva Reddy, Jagjivan Ram would not secure the necessary majority. Indira now pledged her support to Charan Singh and the President was satisfied he could get a majority. So Charan Singh was designated India's prime minister. Indira now played her hand when the vote of confidence in the new government was being moved in Parliament. She withdrew her support and toppled Charan Singh. Fresh elections thus became necessary and in the meanwhile Charan Singh was asked to head a caretaker government.

The Janata Party, thus, collapsed like a pack of cards. The bizarre amalgam of heterogeneous groups and ideologies that had come together on the basis of a common hatred for Indira and the excesses and atrocities of the Emergency disintegrated. At the *samadhi* of Mahatma Gandhi in Rajghat, the former constituents of the party, the Congress (O), the Congress for Democracy (CFD), the Bharatiya Lok Dal (BLD), the Jana Sangh and the Socialists had pledged to leave their past behind, burn their bridges and merge their identities in a common effort to usher in an era of Gandhian socialism that would reach out to the lowliest and the lost. At the end of the 70s, it became clear that the Janata experiment had failed and that the enormous fund of goodwill it had won had been squandered within three years.

True, the Janata Party's achievements during this time were not magnificient. It put democracy back on the rails and dismantled the coercive apparatus of the Emergency. Most of its economic schemes, however, failed to get off the ground because it did not have a broad enough grassroots base to enthuse people and get them involved. Moreover, it did nothing about land reforms or redeeming its promise to provide 10 million jobs in five years. The total revolution of Jayaprakash Narayan was forgotten in the anxiety to maintain the status quo. What was worse, almost from the start, at no time did the Janata Party act as a single unit. Between them, the BLD and the Jana Sangh exercised effective control over the northern states, but soon enough suspicion arose that conspiracy was afoot and the clash of egos of the top Janata Party leaders ended in the party's disintegration.

THIRTY-FOUR

Indira Returns

Indira Gandhi's runaway victory at the general elections in 1980 completely baffled the political pundits. With 351 of the 525 Lok Sabha seats going to her party, she secured a clear two-thirds majority that enabled her to bulldoze her way through the Constitution. No one anticipated such a result. Most commentators were ready to give her only a simple majority with the Janata Party and the Lok Dal following not very far behind.

The popular mood before the elections was one of extreme apathy. Disgusted with all politicians and all parties, the only choice before the electorate was of the lesser of the evils. Many could not make up their minds and stayed away from the hustings. The slightly lower turnout was expected to go in favour of Indira. Even so, many thought, it would be with a simple majority that she would stage a comeback, and she would need the help of other parties to form a government. The future for the country looked bleak, governments toppling one after another as alliances were made or unmade.

The pundits tried to sort out why their predictions failed. But one thing was obvious. Indira took no chances. For her the elections were a question of survival. The commissions set up to inquire the excesses committed by her during Emergency made a powerful case against her. The Maruti small-car project had been shown as a big hoax, involving mother and son in shady deals and the arrests made during the Emergency had been proved to be illegal. The stakes in the elections, were, therefore, high. It was now or never.

In a sense, her election campaign was launched on the day she lost the 1977 elections. Her one objective during their two-and-a-half years in the wilderness was to bring down the Janata Party government, principally by adding fuel to the fire of its internal divisions and preventing it from working effectively. How much the deterioration in the law and order situation or the industrial, caste and communal strife in the country was due to her machinations could not, perhaps, be determined, but obviously she made a capital out of it.

She went all out not only to retain her hold on the affections of the people, but also to increase it. Wherever there was a tragedy, whether floods or drought, wherever there were riots, whether between Hindus and Muslim or Dalits and caste Hindus, there was Indira offering consolation and often her help, whereas, the Janata leaders appeared on the scene either too late or never. Naturally, people responded with equal sympathy to her own tales of the suffering she had to endure from the numerous commissions the government had appointed to go into her and her son's misdeeds. She posed as a martyr and a victim of vendetta and the people soon forgot the forced sterilisation and the mass arrests of the Emergency and lavished their compassion on her.

The Janata Party, on the other hand, were so preoccupied with their internal squabbles and the pursuit of their selfish ambitions that they played foolishly into her hands. The record of the Janata government in putting democracy back on the rails and containing inflation was not insignificant but it failed to meet the rising expectations of the people and project the image of a performing government.

Indeed, the biggest blunder of a large section of the Janata Party was to imagine that with the departure of Devraj Urs, Indira's trusted lieutenant, the spectre of her return was forever laid and they could afford to walk out of the Janata Party and bring down Morarji Desai's government, dominated as it was by the Hindu revivalist RSS. The expected exodus from the Congress-I in the wake of Devraj's exit never took place. Indira wrested the initiative, first by offering to support Charan Singh in the formation of a new government and then by immediately withdrawing the offer, thus toppling him and making fresh elections necessary. Had those elections been held soon after, the pendulum would not have swung so completely in her favour, but four months of Charan Singh's caretaker government were enough to reduce the economy to shambles and land the country in a mess.

Once elections were called, Indira swung into action. Into her campaign, she poured not only her inexhaustible personal resources of energy and drive, but also her equally inexhaustible resources of men and money. Money power played a vital role in Indian elections and every candidate had to invest large sums if he were not to lose his deposit. Money was needed to commandeer a fleet of jeeps fitted with loudspeakers to shout the slogans, and for posters and hoardings, and publicity in the newspapers. Money was also needed to fill the pockets of those who controlled the vote banks, the headmen in slum or village who could guarantee that the entire block voted for a certain candidate or party. As on former occasions, Indira went on her whirlwind tour by helicopter, covering 40 thousand miles in 63 days and visiting 384 constituencies. She delivered as many as 20 speeches a day and drew crowds wherever she went.

She asked her audiences some very elementary questions. How much, she asked, had they to pay for onions or kerosene or sugar and when they replied it was Rs 5 a kilogram or that kerosene or sugar were not available she wanted to know why they should pay so much when onions were a rupee a kilogram and kerosene and sugar were freely available some time ago.

Food and the basic necessities of life touch people very clearly and deeply. Indira had lost the 1977 elections because of forced sterilisation. She won the 1980 elections mainly because of high prices. At bottom this was an onion and kerosene election, not a choice between democracy and dictatorship as the Janata Party wanted the people to believe. Hungry people were angry people and in no mood to make allowances. The government might not have been entirely to blame for one of the worst droughts in recent history or for the double digit inflation that had hit the economy as a result of the oil price hikes. Perhaps, a great deal of the scarcity was artificially created by vested parties, but at election time the blame falls on the government.

A second consideration put before the people by Indira, which weighed heavily with them, was that of law and order. Next to food what people wanted was security and when they heard of murders and robberies committed in broad daylight as in the streets of Delhi or of atrocities against minorities and Dalits as in Jamshedpur or Andhra Pradesh, or of police firing on riotous mobs as in Assam, they wanted a strong hand at the wheel and in this matter both the Janata and the Lok Dal governments had proved to be woefully inadequate.

Faced with these imperatives of food and law and order, the electorate seemed to have forgiven Indira Gandhi her Emergency excesses. In her manifesto that there would be no coercion whatsoever in the family planning campaign. What the country needed and wanted was a leader who would rule with a firm hand in the tradition of Jawaharlal Nehru or even earlier of the British rulers. A largely uneducated and illiterate electorate could hardly think in terms of real democracy and the Indian people, in spite of 30 years of Independence, had ingrained in them the habit of looking to the government as their father and mother, their *ma-baap*. Jayaprakash Narayan's ideas of total revolution and devolution and democracy at the grassroots could not survive after his death 8 October 1979.

In the end, the election turned out to be a referendum for the choice of a prime minister for the country. The answer could be only one: Indira Gandhi. She towered head and shoulders above the rest. In comparison with her, Morarji Desai could be dismissed as a stubborn, old faddist; Charan Singh as a provincial politician with a restricted vision; and Jagjivan Ram as a clever opportunist who would jump on any bandwagon if he could become prime minister. 'The Congress (I) is the only party,' declared the manifesto, 'and Indira Gandhi is the only leader who can save the country after its recent traumatic experience. No other party or leader can be trusted to do so.' The country believed that and voted accordingly. The future would show whether the promise would be kept.

THIRTY-FIVE

1980, Indira's Bid
on Healing Touch

In January 1980, Indira Gandhi returned to power after nearly three years in the wilderness. Disenchanted with the squabbling Janata Party politicians, the country had asked her to come back, giving her Congress (I) party a massive two-thirds majority in Parliament. Indira Gandhi was magnanimous in triumph. 'We are not small and petty minded,' she said when the election results were declared, 'and we do not think in terms of vendetta.'

Assuming office as prime minister on 14 January 1980, Indira Gandhi declared: 'Our country needs the healing touch. We must all unite in a common effort to solve the problems of different sections of our people and different regions of our country.' The Emergency was to be erased from memory. Not in a thousand years, she said, would the need arise for another emergency. She would give the country a government that worked.

Looking at the balance sheet 12 months later, the impression was that Indira's was a government that shirked. None of the promises she made were fulfilled. Inflation was up by 30 per cent and basic commodities had disappeared into the black market where sugar was available at Rs18 a kilogram whereas the controlled price was Rs 3. The number of educated unemployed in the official registers was as high as 15 million. The economy crippled because of basic defects in the infrastructure. There was an acute power shortage, with coal in short supply and the transport system insufficient to carry the load. As a result, agricultural production dropped by 10 per cent and industrial production by 1 per cent. Imports were far in excess of exports. Inflation and high prices had hurt especially the poor and there were riots and demonstration against the price rise in Bombay, Gujarat and Orissa. In Maharashtra and Uttar Pradesh, farmers were agitating for higher procurement prices for their produce, thus pushing up still higher the prices of sugar, rice and coarse grains even in the deplorable public distribution system.

Law and order had broken down. The crime rate shot up. Thefts and murders were frequent occurrences in the trains, atrocities on women were on the increase and Bombay was fast becoming another Delhi where life was insecure even in the daytime. In Bihar, police ganged up with dacoits and landlords in fighting the demands of the landless and the tribals.

It was in Bihar that the infamous Bhagalpur blindings took place in 1980. In the name of law and order, the Bihar police took law and order into their own hands and brutally and brazenly gouged the eyes of 16 undertrial prisoners. If the *Indian Express* and other newspapers had not splashed the news on their front pages, the authorities in the state and the Centre would have sat on earlier complaints and reports. The tragedy was that instead of being horrified by the blindings, the Youth Wing of the Congress and a section of the public in Bihar rushed to the defence of the erring policemen.

Atrocities against lower castes, tribals and minorities took a fearful toll of several hundreds of lives. In Moradabad, a pig strayed into the mosque compound where Muslims were praying on the Id festival day and a pitched battle ensued between them and the police in which over 100 people died. From Moradabad, the fires of communal hatred spread to five other towns, resulting in more arrests and more killings.

It was in Assam and North-East that Indira's government displayed a complete lack of imagination in dealing with the situation. The Assam agitation, in early 1981, had extended to over a year. There seemed no solution. There had been strikes and picketing, and public life had come to a standstill.

The economy of the state and also of the country had suffered because of the oil blockade. But, no imaginative action had been taken by the government to calm the fears of the Assamese, who had been reduced to second-class citizens in their own state and swamped by an overwhelming number of foreigners from Nepal and Bangladesh.

The detection, deletion from the electoral polls and deportation of these foreigners was what the Assamese were agitating for, but Indira did nothing to convince the students who were in the vanguard of this non-violent struggle that their demands were being taken seriously. Towards the mid-80s, this tribal resentment at the influx of foreigners, which had reached such intensity in Assam, spread to Tripura. It took a violent turn, resulting in a battle with the government in which, according to some estimates, five thousand people were massacred.

Instead of going to the root of the problem, both the state and the central governments blamed the troubles in the North-East on missionaries acting as agents for foreign governments. As a result, churches were burnt, mission stations destroyed and missionaries harassed. Their phones were tapped and letters opened in the post. Voluntary agencies like the Little Sisters of the Poor, the St. Vincent de Paul Society, Oxfam and US Catholic Relief Services were excluded from certain tribal areas. Mother Teresa's Missionaries of Charity also came under the ban but was allowed to continue its work when it was pointed out that they were looking after leprosy patients.

Over the whole country then, there hung an air of helplessness. Indira Gandhi blamed the Opposition, though how an Opposition so decimated and fragmented could be responsible for all the mess was more than one could understand. The Janata Party split into five splinter groups. Political parties may have exploited some of the movements and agitations, but as in the farmers agitation in Maharashtra and the students movement in Assam cases, the opposition to the government came increasingly from mass movements that tried to steer clear of political parties, all of which had been so thoroughly discredited.

Twelve months later, the overall records of Indira's government, after her return, was of non-performance. Worse, she seemed bent on arrogating to herself so much power that the country seemed to be teetering on the brink of another Emergency. Towards the end of 1980, during the winter session of Parliament, a National Security Act was passed. It gave the authorities power to detain a person without trial for three months or even a year on the suspicion that he was a danger to the security of the country.

Coming as it did shortly after police had gouged out the eyes of 16 prisoners under trial in Bhagalpur, the National Security Act seemed to place unlimited power in the wrong hands. Even Home Minister Giani Zail Singh admitted that it was identical with the hated Maintenance of Internal Security Act (MISA), on the strength of which thousands of people, including men like Jayaprakash Narayan, were arrested and imprisoned before and during the Emergency. During the same winter session, after a pointless debate on whether the country should switch over to a Presidential system of government, a chorus of voices clamoured for a reimposition of the Emergency, without Indira making the slightest effort to silence her overzealous supporters.

How then did the country come to such a sorry pass? One of the slogans on which Indira came to power was stability, but within weeks nine state assemblies where non-Congress (I) governments were in power were dissolved. Soon after, she succeeded in persuading the Haryana chief minister and his colleagues to defect to the Congress (I) and started the toppling game in West Bengal, Mizoram and Nagaland.

On assuming office, Indira talked about reconciliation and the healing touch, but within weeks she overhauled the whole administrative apparatus arbitrarily dismissing or transferring civil servants who had worked with the previous government or given evidence before the commissions trying Emergency excesses.

Needless to say, all the special courts, commission and probe panels, like the one inquiring into the great Maruti small car hoax were wound up. What was still more astonishing was that the very people who had been indicted by the commissions were promoted to top positions in the civil service or police. Loyalty and closeness to herself or her son Sanjay were the criteria for appointments. Naturally, all this led to a dearth of talent in the government and demoralisation in the administration.

At the same time, a concerted effort was made to build Sanjay Gandhi. In Parliament, he already had 60 MPs, obstreperous muscle men, who shouted down Opposition speakers whenever they got up to make a point. Even in the Cabinet, he had his close confidants like Giani Zail Singh, who had been indicted by the Singh Commission on charges of nepotism and corruption, stand by him. At first, the idea was to make Sanjay chief minister of Uttar Pradesh, but since this would have led to too much public exposure, he was allowed to carry on his back seat driving by having a greater say in party affairs. Older Congressmen resented the strong-arm tactics of Sanjay and his men, but Sanjay was able to crush all opposition by replacing the older men with his younger followers. Eventually, no important decision was taken, even at the state level, without chief ministers dashing off to Delhi and talking it over with both the mother and the son. Credit for the successful outcome of the state assembly elections in May 1980 went to Sanjay and it was taken for granted that he would be the next prime minister. But then came his Icarus-like plunge to death while he was stunt flying over Delhi in his Pitts acrobatic plane. Indira Gandhi was now left completely alone. Whichever way she turned she could find nobody on whom she could rely for advice or even competence. Top Cabinet posts, like that of defence minister, were left unfilled. At first it, was thought Sanjay's wife Maneka Gandhi would take his place but later Indira's other son Rajiv Gandhi seemed to be filling the breach.

By the end of the year, even those more sympathetic towards Indira admitted that there was a crisis. She still retained her charisma and popular appeal and there was no other leader worth writing home about. But she had lost her grip and nerve. The country was in the doldrums, the gap between rich and poor was widening, and the exploited seemed in no mood to allow themselves to be exploited any further. Indira was unable to meet the challenge of their rising expectations, except by hitting out blindly at the opposition and concentrating more power in her hands. She continued to give a government that existed, but not a government that performed.

THIRTY-SIX

Shades of the Emergency

Pavement dwellers are an eyesore. Their hideous hovels disfigure
the landscape and are a disgrace to a thriving metropolis. In one
of the heaviest downpours of the monsoon in September 1981,
demolition squads swooped down on some 10 thousand of them
on a six-mile stretch of road in the heart of Bombay's mill area
and another three-mile stretch near the airport. Armed with an
executive fiat, they battered those pitifully inadequate shelters of
tin and burlap to the ground and scattered the pavement dwellers
meagre possessions to the winds.

It was only late in the day that operations were halted. An irate
high court judge dismissed as sanctimonious nonsense, the government's plea that it was for the benefit of the victims that their huts
were destroyed. It passed a stay order terminating operations till
the end of the rains in October. Meanwhile, the damage had been
done. Not a single hut remained standing and a thousand occupants

were herded into state transport buses and driven to destinations hundreds of miles away that most had left years ago and many had never known. Worse was the plight of those who stayed back. For at least three days, the homeless were chased by the city police on to the platforms of railway stations and from the stations back to the sodden streets by the railway police. Compassion was abandoned. The parents of a child stricken with chickenpox begged that their hut be spared. But no, orders were orders. The child died, a victim of man's insensitivity to the sufferings of others.

Doubtless, the pavement dwellers' miserable hovels were a health hazard, not the least to themselves. But Bombay's immense population in 1981 of 8.5 million included 3.5 million slum dwellers. They lived in equally squatted and unhygienic conditions.

The Bombay demolitions were harshly reminiscent of those at Delhi's Turkman Gate during the Emergency. Indeed, there was a growing feeling that shades of the Emergency were closing about the country. The National Security Act had given the government the power to imprison anyone thought to be a danger to the security of the country. The Essential Services Maintenance Ordinance now effectively banned all strikes and took away from workers their right to collective bargaining. It affected all wage earners from government officials to taxi drivers. Almost any industrial establishment or public utility service could be declared essential. Not only could strikes now be forbidden but also the encouragement of others to strike, or the refusal to work overtime. Any policeman on reasonable suspicion could arrest a worker without warrant and have him jailed for six months or fined a thousand rupees after a summary trial.

The Ordinance took most people by surprise. The number of strikes had decreased from 2,117 in 1978 to 255 in 1981. Man-days lost had declined from 43 million in 1979 to 13 million in 1980 nearly half of those from lockouts and layoffs. Industrial relations had entered a halcyon period. Why then the Ordinance? The only explanation was that it was a pre-emptive move to snuff out labour unrest in the wake of spiralling prices. Admittedly the economy was in deep trouble. Inflation was at 18 per cent and there was a staggering budgetary as well as balance of payments deficit.

In a year of bumper harvests, wheat was being imported from the United States. Fuel had been added to the inflationary fires by an increase in petroleum prices and in import duties on edible oils. Prices of essential goods were, therefore, bound to increase sharply. So, before they did rise and before workers demanded higher wages or otherwise struck, the Ordinance cut the ground under their feet. In effect, the Ordinance meant a wage freeze.

It was not surprising, therefore, that the ordinance was welcomed by big business and industry. Indeed, the absence of any mention of lockouts and layoffs suggested collision between government and capital and the embarking on a deliberate policy of repression of the workers with scant regard for democratic norms and procedures. Any labour legislation could well have waited for the opening of Parliament's Monsoon session two weeks later. The Ordinance, therefore, aroused resentment and anger on the part of workers. About 12 thousand of them marched to Parliament on 18 August when it was to reopen and demanded that the 'Black law' be scrapped. They also warned that if the law was not scrapped, there would be another march of hundreds of thousands of workers in November and a countrywide general strike would be called for, whatever the consequences. It would mark the beginning of a new movement for freedom.

THIRTY-SEVEN

Indira and the Pope's Rosary

The great majority of those affected by the Bombay demolitions were the poorest of the poor and caste-wise the lowest of the low. In India, caste and class are largely synonymous and together with creed form the lines along which society is divided. It is true that since industrialisation, class has begun to play a larger role, but caste still retains its traditional hold. All over the country members of the lowest caste or Dalits are still regarded subhuman, forced to remove their shirts and footwear when walking the public streets, secluded in ghettoes in towns and villages and forbidden to draw water from the village tank or well. Poor, illiterate and landless, they have their houses burnt and their women raped if they dare claim their lawful rights. The only difference is that those who oppress them are no longer the Brahmins at the top of the hierarchical ladder but the landlords, moneylenders, merchants and industrialists of the middle and higher middle classes and castes.

Early in 1981, a sleepy village in south India, called Meenakshipuram, suddenly made the headlines. A thousand Hindu Dalits converted to Muslims. Some thousand others in scattered places in Tamil Nadu followed them. The mass conversions sent shock waves in the Hindu society. A little later rumours spread that some 25 thousand Dalits in north India were getting ready to give up their faith and embrace another. What was happening? The Hindus were alarmed that their religion was in danger and that if the exodus were not arrested the country might wake up to find itself Islamic. Rumours had it that petro-dollars were pouring in from the Gulf countries in a concerted attempt to Islamise the 80 million Dalits. The Hindu leaders accordingly made a dash for Meenakshipuram to find out what went wrong. Union Minister of State, Swaminathan, paid a flying visit to the 'affected areas' and stated categorically that Dalits were paid to convert to Islam.

Reformist Hindu organisations, like the Ramakrishna Mission and the Arya Samaj, appealed to Dalits not to leave the fold and to other Hindus to treat them with brotherly love. Atal Behari Vajpayee, leader of the biggest Opposition party, the BJP, went down to the village and organised a dinner for the 50 Dalits who had reconverted to Hinduism. The Tamil Nadu government ordered a public inquiry and O P Tyagi, of Freedom of Religion Bill fame, called for a ban on conversions.

The whole series of incidents had probably been blown out of proportion. Union Home Minister Giani Zail Singh announced that since February only two thousand people had converted to Islam. Politicians were quick to get on to the act and exploit the conversions for their own purposes.

The truth is that even the most cowed and subservient human beings can take only so much and no more of the contumely, the insults and the economic and social deprivation that are the characteristics of the caste system. Meenakshipuram was a sign that even the worm could turn and that the oppressed and depressed classes and castes of Indian society were waking up to their rights and human dignity as the revolution of rising expectations began to reach the remotest corners of India.

After the Muslims came the turn of the Christians. Nagercoil and Kanyakumari at the tip of the Indian peninsula had been for years peaceful districts where Hindus and Christians had mingled freely and fraternised with each other. Twenty years back, there was a stray incident when a cross was removed from the islet near Kanyakumari and the place renamed Vivekananda Rock after the Swami, who is said to have meditated there. In February 1982, after a conference for Christian Unity, the Hindus too held a conference for Hindu unity in Nagercoil, organised by the Vishwa Hindu Parishad and the RSS.

Inflammatory speeches were made against Christians, terror and violence broke loose and in the resulting blood bath some people, nearly all Christians, were killed. When the matter came up in the Rajya Sabha, all three main speakers, Margaret Alva (Congress-S), Kalyansundaram (CPI) and Harikishan Singh Surjeet (CPI-M) were agreed that wherever the Vishwa Hindu Parishad went, riots broke out. Surjeet said he had information that the two local RSS leaders had a task force of 200 hiding in their homes, which at their bidding went about beating, burning and damaging. 'The coastal villages in the area,' reported the *Hindustan Times*, 'present a ghastly sight of religious vendetta. Churches, convents and other property belonging to Christians have been looted and burnt down in an organised manner.' A press release from the Catholic church and Church of South India stated that the RSS had been making the Kanyakumari district a testing ground for their ultimate aim of annihilating Christianity (and Islam) and making India the home of the Hindus alone.

As for Indira, she proudly allowed herself to be photographed making offerings at some of the Hindu shrines and temples. 'It would, however,' writes Hari Jaisingh in *India between Myth and Reality,* 'be unfair to dub Indira's identification with Hinduism as a sheer gimmick. It should be recognised that, in the face of her growing personal problems, she began to lean towards the Hindu thought and practice.'

Be that as it may, her meeting with Pope John Paul II in Rome towards the end of 1981 had special significance. By all accounts it was a cordial one. Though the Holy Father had not quite recovered from his operation after the assassination attempt on his life and consequently gave a limited number of interviews, the fact that an interview with the Indian prime minister was included, showed the great importance the Vatican and India placed on their mutual relations. The interview lasted for half-an-hour, which in the Pope's condition could be considered long. Though no communiqué was issued, according to the *Times of India,* she talked about world peace and spirituality.

Indira had stopped in Rome on her way back to India from the Cancun Summit on Poverty. She was reported to have given the Pope a wood carving of the Last Supper and the Pope, in turn, gave her a rosary. Indira, as a young girl, had taken tuitions in Latin and French from Bishop Conrad De Vito of Lucknow and the gift must have recalled to her memory the large rosary that as a Capuchin hung from the cord round his waist.

Earlier, when Pope Paul VI had visited India, she had been there along with Prime Minister Lal Bahadur Shastri at the airport in Bombay to welcome him. Also, when presenting an award to Mother Teresa, she had said that she felt humbled in the presence of someone for whom 'The giving was all.'

THIRTY-EIGHT

Blood Bath in Assam

Communal, linguistic, caste and class conflicts have caused streams of blood to flow ever since India became independent, but not since the terrible aftermath of the Partition had the country witnessed such scenes as took place during the elections in Assam in February 1983.

Day after day, Press reports told of bombing and assault, of arson and loot, of kidnapping and mayhem, of entire villages burning to the ground, and of locals butchering migrants and migrants paying locals back in kind. Casualties mounted ominously until on Friday, 18 February, in one appalling massacre, a thousand people were liquidated in a camp near a town called Nellie. Pitched battles were fought with bows and arrows and firearms and corpses littered the fields on the banks of Brahmaputra.

The spark that set Assam aflame was the decision to hold elections, but the cause and object of this outpouring of hatred were the successive waves of immigrants who threatened to make the

Assamese a minority in their own land. Even before Independence, a large numbers of people used to be brought from Bihar and Orissa to work in the tea gardens. After Independence, when plans were made for the development of the state, hordes of Bengalis from West Bengal descended upon Assam to capture the plum jobs. Assamese, though by then educated and awakened, were reduced to being hewers of wood and drawers of water. To make matters worse, from 1951 onwards, thousands of Muslims, from then East Pakistan, infiltrated across the border and with the creation of Bangladesh, this influx became a flood.

Some differences were narrowed. The Assamese agreed that immigrants who had come before 1961 could remain. The government proposed 1971 as the cut-off date. The fate of the immigrants who had entered between these two dates defied solution.

The impasse had not been resolved when it was decided to hold elections. The government argued, not quite convincingly, that Presidential rule on the state could not be extended. Indira expected to benefit from the votes of the immigrants.

That democratic elections were an impossibility, under the circumstances, should have been obvious. The electoral registers were four years old and not only had they not been brought up to date, they also included, according to an Assamese leader, the name of 20 lakh (two million) foreign nationals.

The Assamese leaders had warned after the breakdown of the talks with the government, that if elections were held, the initiative might well pass to extremists who would not desist from violence. (They themselves had adhered strictly to the Gandhian methods of non-violence and *Satyagraha*). It would seem that a commission sent to inquire about the prospects for holding elections reported that there would be no problem. In fact, it was a highly inflammable situation, which only the local leaders knew.

The main opposition parties and leaders of the Assamese people's movement decided to boycott the elections as soon as they were announced. The government responded by arresting the militants and the student leaders under the National Security Act and forbidding the Press from publishing any reports abut the anti-election campaign. The entire personnel to conduct the elections had to be recruited from outside the state as the local people refused to have anything to do with the election machinery. Fifty battalions of armed police from all over the country, including the dreaded Provisional Armed Constabulary (PAC) from Uttar Pradesh were pressed into service for supervising the elections. It was a democratic elections at the gunpoint.

As things turned out, the vast majority of Assamese boycotted the polls. In areas where they were dominant, not a single voter was willing or able to cast his vote. Quite as predictably, where migrants or long-settled Bengalis and Muslims were in the majority, the results were exactly the opposite with 'outsiders' voting en masse and the locals conspicuous by their absence. Indira's Congress (I) party won a landslide since she and the leading politicians of her Congress (I) Party had campaigned on the platform that they alone could guarantee the security of the minorities.

But it was a pyrrhic victory, worse than defeat. Indira Gandhi had set her heart on holding and winning the elections in Assam so that, together with her victory in the New Delhi elections, it would offset the catastrophic rout of her party in Andhra Pradesh and Karnataka. The two erstwhile bastions should have fallen was a vote of censure against a party that promised a 'government that works' but instead spent its time in intrigue, squabbling and the peddling of patronage.

The Assam victory could only provide cold comfort. The government thrown up by this travesty of an election had no claims to legitimacy and would be rejected by the Assamese. Heavy deployment of the army might ultimately restore a semblance of peace. The elections did not bring any answer to Assam's problems. It only worsened them. Feelings had been exacerbated and the Assamese people felt alienated. This beautiful but troubled state on India's sensitive North-East frontier had become a boiling cauldron that could spill over to the entire area on the borders of China.

THIRTY-NINE

Hindus On the March

Not since the eighth century, perhaps, had India witnessed such scenes of religious fervour as during the *Ekatmata Yatra* (pilgrimage for one soul or solidarity) at the end of 1983. Between 16 November and 16 December three mighty processions walked through the land — one from Kathmandu in Nepal to Rameshwaram in South India, another in the same direction from Haridwar (now in Uttrakhand region) to Kanyakumari at the southernmost tip and the third from Gangasagar near Calcutta in the east to Dwarka in the west.

Two richly ornamented chariots bearing thousands of litres of Ganges water in an eight feet high brass vessel and a shining metal image of *Bharat Mata* or Mother India formed the centrepiece of each of these three processions. It was as though three immensely long rivers, fed by innumerable tributaries — for 97 smaller processions joined at various points — were flooding the land. Along many routes saffron-coloured flags were waved in welcome. At the end of each day, the chariots stopped and were festooned with garlands and petals, speeches were delivered, thousands of bottles of Ganges water sold, books and pamphlets were distributed and exhibitions held extolling the glories of Hinduism and Hindustan.

No fair-minded Indian could have had any quarrel with the aims of the *Yatra* (pilgrimage). Hinduism is an amorphous and pluralistic system, riven by divisions and sects and plagued with the evils of the caste system. The organisers said they wanted to unite the Hindus by instilling a sense of pride in their ancient heritage and culture deriving from the Vedas and other scriptures. That the *yatra* should have brought together religious leaders from different Hindu persuasions was a measure of the accord of one soulness arrived at. The organisers claimed that 10 crore people were involved in the pilgrimage — a sure indication that Hinduism still commanded a hold in the hearts of the Indian masses.

Again, no fair-minded Indian could have had any quarrel with the symbols chosen for this manifestation of Hindu piety. Together with the Nile in Egypt and the Euphrates and Tigris in Mesopotamia, the Ganges was the centre of a great ancient river civilisation. Arising in the Himalayas, descending to the plains at Rishikesh and then flowing eastwards to empty its waters in the Bay of Bengal, the Ganges or Ganga brought life and fertility to the vast north Indian plain. So much of India's history and culture, so much of the mythology and sacred writings revolved round the Ganga that quite naturally the river came to be called *Ganga Mata* or Mother Ganges. Non-Hindus, therefore, can easily understand why the river is held in such great affection and reverence by Hindus and why the organisers of the *yatra* should want similar respect to be paid to it by others.

Affection and esteem are one thing. Quite another was the demand that all Indians, even non-Hindus, should call the river

Mother, regard her as a deity to be worshipped and presumably adore her or forfeit their claim to be Indians. Similarly, love for the country and pride in its ancient heritage and culture should be part of the psychology of any Indian. It was quite another matter to expect non-Hindus to worship an eight feet image of *Bharat Mata* riding a lion in triumph or reclining on tigers.

Yet that was precisely what the Vishwa Hindu Parishad (The All Hindu Assembly) that organised the *yatra* wanted and did. 'Let me make it very clear,' said its secretary general, 'that the *yatra* is for those who accept this land as their motherland. Only the Hindus call this land *Bharat Mata*. The others do not.' Not just names but a whole attitude to India's past lay behind this identification of India with Hinduism.

According to two pamphlets distributed during the *yatras*, the last millennium was an enormous blot on India's history, leaving behind three monstrous evils: Islam, Christianity and Macaulayism (an umbrella term for the English language and Western liberal thought). These had to be purged.

What rankled most deeply in the minds of the organisers was Partition and the ghastly killings that accompanied it. By the sword, the foreign invaders had retained possession of part of the sacred body of *Bharat Mata*, which they had already grossly violated before. Pakistan, Bangladesh and even Afghanistan must, therefore, be reacquired by India. Pride of place during the *Yatra* was given to portraits not of Mahatma Gandhi or the leaders of the Independence movement, but of men like Veer Savarkar and Guru Golwalkar who were implicated in Gandhi's murder. Indeed, India's Constitution and national flag counted for little in the eyes of the *yatra's* organisers.

Interviewed by the *Illustrated Weekly of India*, Swami Chin-mayananda, the founder of the Vishwa Hindu Parishad (VHP), declared, 'who cares for the national flag or the national symbol? In 36 years has it integrated the country? The Ganges is sacred to all.' When told that in the name of religion people were killing each other in India, he replied: 'Nature maintains a certain balance' as the Malthusian theory says, 'when the population rises beyond a certain point, nature brings down the level.'

Another of the ostensible purposes of the *yatra* was to rid the Hindu society of the outmoded social traditions like caste and untouchability. Hindu religious leaders made speeches rejecting these obnoxious customs as in no way entailed by Hindu belief or sanctioned by Hindu scriptures. The Shankaracharya of Puri and Dwarka, however, disagreed with this opinion and some people wondered why the Vishwa Hindu Parishad, whose top leadership was confined to Brahmins should suddenly have developed such concern when it had never lifted a finger in the past to prevent the Dalits, or untouchables, from being shamefully treated and even burnt alive. Not only did the VHP have no idea how to bring about emotional integration between Dalits and caste Hindus, it did not even care.

The fact was that the whole idea of the *yatra* originally sprang from the conversion to Islam of a thousand Dalits two-and-a-half ago at Meenakshipuram in the south. That led the VHP to swing back into action steming the tide of Muslim expansion. The conversions, they said, were the result of Arab money from the Gulf. If not stopped, the consequences for Hinduism would be disastrous. Suddenly, Hindu India was awakened to the fact that the Hindu population had declined from 87 to 85 per cent. Muslims and Christians were adding to their numbers by conversions and large families. Hindus would become a minority in the country as they already were in Kashmir, Punjab and north-eastern India.

Christians then became the next target for attack. Ten Christian fishermen were killed and a church, a convent and an entire village was destroyed in Kanyakumari district, following the communal tension, whipped by the VHP, over a petty quarrel on the use of loudspeakers in adjacent Hindu and Christian shrines. Still later, the agitation was carried over to Nilackal in Kerala, where Christians shifted the church to another site because of Hindu objections.

However laudable the aims of the *yatra*, the slogans shouted and the pamphlets distributed showed all too clearly that the real targets were the minority communities. Despite the disclaimers that the pilgrimage had any political connection, VHP has close links with the Rashtriya Swayamsevak Sangh (RSS), the militant Hindu wing of the Bharatiya Janata Party (BJP). The politics of the *yatra* was clear to see when Indira attacked it whereupon the entire BJP leadership, including its aspiring Prime Minister A B Vajpayee pushed to its defence.

Not that Indira's attitude to the *yatra* was consistent. First, there were reports that she had actively encouraged the VHP to organise it. After the Meenakshipuram conversions, she told a delegation of Hindus that it would help to strengthen her hand against such occurrences if they organised themselves. The RSS too in the meantime had developed a favourable attitude towards her. Her posing as a conservative Hindu, visiting temples and holy men and her tough stand against Pakistan were just what they wanted. Her victories in the elections in Delhi and in Jammu convinced her that skilful pandering to Hindu communalism would reap political dividends though friends who wanted India to stay secular had warned her that she was playing with fire. It was only when the *yatra's* organisers refused to take away the posters of Guru Golwalkar that she realised that the political benefits of the *yatra* would go mainly to her opponents. Then, she issued her condemnation but after that she kept a discreet silence, so that many of the Congress members took part in the *yatra* without any qualms. Which way,therefore, the Hindu vote would go was not very clear.

Religion, of course, has always played an important role in India's politics, especially at the time of elections, but never had it been so shamelessly exploited for partisan purposes. The lessons of the Sikh-Hindu warfare in the Punjab and the Hindu-Muslim conflagration in Assam had yet to be learnt. Under the hammer blows of the politics of religion, there was a danger that the values of democracy, secularism and socialism, written into our Constitution, would be destroyed.

A classic example of the mindlessness of those who exploit religion for their own purposes was the orgy of communal violence that engulfed Bhiwandi and Bombay in May 1984. Sparked by the placing of a garland of *chappals* on the picture of a leader, pitched battles were fought in the cities' streets between hostile mobs confronting each other with soda water bottles, home-made arms and swords. Boulders were hurled at shops and establishments when the call for *bandhs* and the downing of shutters went unheeded. About thirty people were burnt alive in Bhiwandi and the number of people killed in the two cities rose to 150. Bodies of the dead were piled high in the cities' morgues and the maimed and the wounded filled the hospitals to bursting point. The denizens of the underworld had a field day.

The events of those few days left behind not only the stench of rotting bodies, but also deep scars in the collective psyche of both, indeed of all communities that would not easily be healed. As Indira said, they were a terrible blot not only on the name of this city of Bombay, but of the country as well. A terrible responsibility rested on those who made inflammatory speeches or hate-filled gestures that provoked the killings, especially of the poor and downtrodden.

FORTY

Another Monumental Blunder

Religion and politics not only made a heady but also a dangerous mix. Indira's personal tragedy was a result of such circumstances. Few days in the country's post-Independence history were sadder than those in mid June 1984 when the holiest shrine for Sikhs, the Golden Temple in Amritsar, became a battleground in which 500 of its inmates, some priests along with Sant Jarnail Singh Bhindranwale, lost their lives. Even though the Harmandir Sahib, the place in the Golden Temple where the Sikh Scripture is kept for worship, was not touched, the rest of the Golden Temple complex, including the Akal Takht, the seat of the law making body of the Sikhs, was battered and broken. Scores of gurdwaras all over the state were attacked. Those were some of the most painful events for the Sikhs in their history.

That tragedy had something nay almost everything to do with the rise of fundamentalism in religion and the close intertwining of religion with politics. Bhindranwale had the fanatic's fierce look but his charisma was such that he could recite the *Gurbani* in a manner that touched the hearts of the Sikh masses. His call for religious purity was undoubtedly fundamentalist but had a revolutionary appeal that drew support from the student intellectuals of the All India Sikh Students Federation.

Indeed the phenomenon of Blundranwale and the Punjab imbroglio could not properly be understood apart from the crises in Sikhism which reached traumatic proportions with the desecration of the Golden Temple. That shrine symbolized the identity and integrity of Sikhism, which it seemed to be losing under the pressures of modernism. Sikh fundamentalism was a backlash against the slow erosion of Sikh doctrine and the flouting of the moral and disciplinary code of the Khalsa established by the ninth Guru, Guru Tegh Bahadur.

It insisted on the importance of Sikhism as one of the world's great religions, distinct from Hinduism and Islam and providing an alternative to both. Sikh fundamentalism recalled the scattered Sikhs to a sense of solidarity and social cohesiveness, embodied in the *Panth*. This made for religious revival and accounted for the ease with which the Sikh masses in the villages joined the Akali Morcha.

Sikh fundamentalism led to the dangers of sectarianism and intolerance. Certain ideas of the Sikh gurus that had developed in times of persecution like the sacredness of arms and the necessity of a *dharmayuddha* (religious war) came to be emphasised to the detriment of other values like kindness, preached by Guru Nanak. Sikh fundamentalism gave rise to the emergence of fire-eating hot gospellers like Bhindranwale, who armed themselves to the teeth, preached vengeance on the enemies of their religion or those who compromised with them, and engaged in a holy war for the establishment of a Sikh independent state.

Sikhs had been in the vanguard against Partition and left their ancestral homeland en masse along with Hindus. They clung passionately to the Punjabi language and the Gurmukhi Script in which their scriptures were written. They expected the new Punjab state to be drawn on linguistic lines. Instead, the former Punjab was divided into Punjab and Haryana, large tracts of Punjabi speaking villages allotted to Haryana, and Hindi was adopted by the Hindus. Chandigarh, the new capital built by Le Corbusier in place of Lahore, was also divided between Punjab and Haryana and the whole administered as Union Territory. The waters of the five rivers became matters of dispute and even the great hydroelectric projects were brought under the Centre. All these grievances were articulated in the form of demands. But in spite of more than two years of protracted negotiations, no settlement had been reached.

To realise these demands, in May 1982, Sant Harchand Singh Longowal launched the non-violent Akali Morcha. He was upright, moderate and had enough clout to hammer out and honour an agreement. But unsuccessful in his non-violent efforts, he switched over from a politico-secular strategy to a *dharmayuddha* (holy war). His Akali Dal was a politico-regional party but he was the spokesman of the *Panth* and voiced the Sikh interests. Longowal's *morcha* took the form of 'rail aur rasta roko', city and state *bandhs* and the public burning of Article 25 of the Constitution, which bracketed Sikhs with Hindus. He enrolled a hundred thousand volunteers who pledged themselves to do or die for the cause. The entire Sikh community backed the agitation with their latest move stopping food grains from being sent outside the state of Punjab.

To divide the Akalis, the Congress (I) built up Bhindranwale and brought him into the arena of Punjab politics. His meteoric rise upset the older Akali leaders, who found they had to ride on his charisma. Though not even a member of the Akali Dal, he had signed the do or die pledge and became the Dal's back seat driver. His close followers, the members of the All India Sikh Student's Federation criticised Longowal for not being effective and revolutionary enough.

Among his other supporters were retired army officials, civil servants, urban professionals and the masses of Sikh peasants in the villages. At one stage, there was bitter acrimony between Longowal and Bhindranwale but differences were patched up; and they drew up a joint statement calling on all Sikhs to rally behind the *Panth* and fight under the banner of the Akali Dal.

Bhindranwale seemed to have barricaded himself with his followers in the Akal Takht, which was well stocked with the most formidable and sophisticated modern weaponry. In the Akal Takht there was a command group that masterminded the guerilla warfare and had ordered the killings of over 200 people, dacoities and burning of public property, like railway stations, for over two years. The terrorists used hit-and-run tactics, choosing whom to kill and when to kill and getting away without fear of being caught. Their design seemed to have been to terrorise Hindus and dissident Sikhs to leave Punjab free for the establishment of a Sikh religious state.

Indira Gandhi's government tried every means to put an end to these acts of terrorism but to no avail. She dismissed the Darbara Singh Congress (I) ministry and brought the State under President's rule. She declared Punjab to be a disturbed area, then a very disturbed area. She brought in para-military forces like the Special Reserve Police and the Central Reserve Police Force, but the killings and the outrages went on. Finally, her patience seemed to have run out, the army was called in and troops marched into the Golden Temple, killing Bhindranwale and 500 others, pulverising the Akal Takht, which was part of the Sikhs holiest shrine. It was a monumental blunder.

FORTY-ONE

The Final Tragedy

The assault on the Akal Takht, and the whole chain of events in Punjab leading to it, left Indira's shaken. The Sikhs had been the great stalwarts of India's Independence and defence and now they felt completely alienated. No amount of compensation to heal the Sikh psyche. By getting the army and a few Sikh volunteers to repair the temple and the Akal Takht and by calling a worldwide conference of peace-loving Sikhs (who disagreed with the extremists, the Sarbat Khalsa), Indira merely succeeded in dividing the Sikhs and alienating them still further.

Punjab was still under the army rule, thousands of Akalis were in prison. Rare manuscripts of the Sikh scripture were lost and the number of Sikhs killed was never revealed. Sikhs were suspected, searched, discriminated against and persecuted. All this led to the demand for Khalistan, an independent Sikh state.

On 15 August 1984, from the ramparts of Delhi's Red Fort, Indira gave a call for unity. The country, she said, faced a situation in which its survival was in question. To ensure this survival, the country had to unite solidly behind her, close its ranks and give up party differences.

After what the Sikh priests called attempted genocide, Sikh alienation was complete. Even the moderates had turned into extremists. Less than a month after her appeal for unity, she and the country as a whole had to pay the price for Operation Blue Star (1984). She had earlier been advised not to have any Sikhs as her bodyguard. She refused to accept that she could no longer trust members of an Indian community. On 31 October 1984, she was shot down by two of her bodyguards, both Sikhs, in the garden of her house in Delhi.

FORTY-TWO

Things Fall Apart

'Things fall apart, the Centre cannot hold.' Those words of William Butler Yeats, seemed never more appropriate than when a mindless wave of violence swept over a hundred cities and towns of India in the wake of Indira Gandhi's assassination. Marauding crowds rampaged through the streets of Delhi, setting fire to neighbourhoods, attacking temples, destroying property, looting shops and butchering anyone wearing a Sikh turban. More than 1,500 people were killed on one day alone, while the police looked on or even joined in. The whole machinery of government came to a halt. Not until the army, deployed after Indira's funeral swung into action, arresting thousands and moving terror-stricken Sikhs into replacement camps did the fury abate.

Indira Gandhi had been talking incessantly before her death of the need for unity. Given the vastness of the country, thousands of miles in length and breadth, the immensity of its problems, the baffling multiplicity of its languages and castes and creeds and hundreds of local and regional interests, all pulling in different directions, India's Constitution and flag could not in a largely illiterate population evoke the kind of devotion and loyalty that only a charismatic person like Indira could. By all accounts, she was the only person who could hold the country together. Despite all her foibles and failures, she remained the 'darling of the masses' as once her father had been.

Indeed there was no other figure on the Indian national scene like her who was such a farsighted political genius and possessed universal vision and who personified and symbolized India in the eyes of the world. In a very real, but somewhat exaggerated sense, India was Indira and Indira was India. She was one of the major figures in the councils of the world and could hold her own even among the superpower leaders of the world. She took over from her father the leadership of the non- aligned nations.

Her election to the chairmanship of Non Aligned Movement (NAM) on 7 March 1983 being eloquent testimony to this. She was one of the most outstanding spokespersons who cared for the concerns of the Third World developing nations. They were struggling to emerge from the poverty and ignorance that hundred of years of colonialism had enveloped them in and to find a place of equality and dignity and justice in the comity of nations.

In the ongoing North-South dialogue, hers was one of the most persuasive and influential voices. In that sense, she was one of the world's greatest women. Her death was, as Britain's Prime Minister Margot Thatcher described, a 'tragedy for the world.'

Indira's finest hour was in 1971. When she became prime minister in 1965, after the death of Lal Bahadur Shastri, it was as Jawaharlal Nehru's daughter; a compromise candidate among the stalwarts of the Congress, a frail and fragile woman who would do the bidding of her mentors. But she soon showed she had a mind of her own. With the abolition of privy purses, the nationalisation of banks and the election of V V Giri as the President of India, she proved to be more than a match for her rivals, and her campaign of '*Garibi Hatao*' more than an answer to their slogan of '*Indira Hatao*.'

In the mid-term elections of March 1971, she routed the 'Grand Alliance', formed by some of her former rivals in the split Congress Party, won an overwhelming majority of votes and secured a mandate to root out poverty, close the gap between rich and poor and to take the country towards a secular and socialist democracy.

She was now the undisputed leader of the country standing head and shoulders above the others. After the struggle, with the Syndicate behind her, she could rise to the challenge of the Bangladesh crisis and the war that followed. It was here that she showed those qualities of courage and bravery and that capacity for hard work and quick decisions that enabled her to rally the nation behind her and come to the aid of a stricken people who were asserting their right to independence. Thus, a new nation was born and Indira rode the crest of popularity that was even greater than when she had won the elections. Indira was *Bharat's Ratna* in a very real sense.

Her darkest hour was in 1975 when the Allahabad High Court judgment found irregularities in her 1971 election campaign. They may have been technical defects but her obvious duty was to resign. Instead of that she went on to impose Emergency on the country, alter the Constitution and concentrated all powers in her hand. How a great Prime Minister like Indira could impose a dictatorial regime, during which the very right to life and liberty were suspended and a caucas led by her son Sanjay allowed to carry out a mindless forced sterilisation campaign is one of the great enigmas of history. Perhaps it was too close an identification of her personal interests with those of the country. The result was predictable. She was rejected in the elections by the very people who loved her, and to whom she had given her affection.

She staged a marvellous comeback within three years after the failure of the Janata Party, winning the subsequent elections with an overwhelming majority.

The last four years were a troubled time for the country with violence erupting in Bombay, Bhiwandi, Kerala and Tamil Nadu and then on a massive scale in Assam and Punjab. The country was falling apart and there seemed to be no way of holding it together.

It was then that Indira made her second monumental blunder by ordering the assault on the Golden Temple and pulverising the Akal Takht. Barely two months after she had made an appeal for unity, she was shot down by her own Sikh bodyguards. She could not live to realise her dream of a unity and secured India. Whatever her failures and weaknesses, she delivered her best to the land she loved. India will remember her with affection and gratitude.

Bibliography

1. *India Between Dream and Reality* by Hari Jaisingh. Allied Publishers, Bombay, New Delhi, 1989.
2. *The Indian Triumvirate* A political biography of Gandhi, Patel and Nehru by V. B. Kulkarni. Bharatiya Vidya Bhavan, Bombay, 1969.
3. *From Raj to Rajiv* 40 years of Indian Independence by Mark Tully and Zareer Masani. Universal Book Stall, New Delhi, 1988.
4. *The End of an Era* The Rise and Fall of Indira Gandhi by C.S. Pandit. Allied Publishers, Bombay, 1977.
5. *No Kin to the Mahatma* A Study of Indira Gandhi by Susanna Heredia. Vantage Press, New York, 1977.
6. *Is J.P. the Answer* by Minoo Masani. Macmillan Company of India, Delhi, Bombay, 1975.
7. *Experiment with Untruth* India Under the Emergency by Michael Henderson. Macmillan, India, 1975.
8. *Indira Gandhi*—Speeches and Writings. Harper and Row, Evanston, London, 1974.

9. *The Guru in Sikhism* by W. Owen Cole. Darton, Longman and Todd, London, 1982.

10. *Sikhism in its Indian Context 1469–1708* by W. Owen Cole. Darton, Longman and Todd, London, 1983.

Index